Main

"*O Great One!* is by far the best book on the power of recognition that I have ever read. It will make a difference not only in your life but also in the lives of people you interact with at work, at home, and in your community."

—Ken Blanchard, coauthor of
The New One Minute Manager® and *Collaboration Begins with You*

"David Novak built YUM! into a great company by bringing out the best in his people. *O Great One!* shows you how easy it is to help people reach their potential. He is a great storyteller!"

—Rick Pitino, head basketball coach, University of Louisville

"After you devour this thoroughly enjoyable page-turner, buy it for all the leaders and future leaders in your life. It'll make a huge difference!"

—Bob Burg, coauthor of *The Go-Giver* and *The Go-Giver Leader*

"David Novak hit another home run with *O Great One!* His message is clear: when we take care of our people, they take care of everything else."

—John Calipari, head basketball coach, University of Kentucky

"This heartwarming story will captivate your spirit and challenge your leadership philosophy. Nobody has more credibility to deliver this message than David, who regularly uses the magic of recognition to lead his teams to extraordinary success."

—Steve Reinemund, former chairman and CEO, PepsiCo

"No one understands the power of recognition more and has translated it into tangible results better than David Novak. He is the world's authority on recognition."

—Mike Rawlings, Mayor of Dallas

"The valuable lessons and insights shared in *O Great One!* should be applied to achieve powerful results not only in your business but with your family." —Brian Cornell, Chairman and CEO, Target

"*O Great One!*" is an easy read that hits the nail on the head. Successful companies are all about people and this book proves that people work more effectively when they are appreciated and recognized for their contributions to team success."

—Dr. Bob Rotella, psychologist and performance consultant

"Throughout his career, David has employed these same principles of recognition to drive terrific results. It works."

—David Cote, Chairman and CEO, Honeywell

"*O Great One!* is a sweet story that contains a very important lesson: recognition is the key to creating an open and successful organization."

—Jamie Dimon, Chairman and CEO, JPMorgan Chase

"I thank David Novak for writing a powerful book that was not only fun to read but provided valuable management lessons. I completely support these ten guiding principles. Leaders in every field should read *O Great One!* and embrace the power of recognition!"

—Terry Lundgren, President & CEO, Macy's, Inc.

"This uplifting story reminds us that praise, recognition, and encouragement are key to transforming the human spirit. A truly inspiring book."

—Massimo Ferragamo, chairman at Ferragamo USA

"*O Great One!* is not only a wonderful and engaging story but one with countless teachable moments that can be learned from and put into practice."

—Noel Tichy, professor, Ross School of Business,
University of Michigan, author of *Succession* and coauthor
of *Judgment on the Front Line* (with Chris DeRose)

O GREAT ONE!

O GREAT ONE!

A Little Story About the Awesome
Power of Recognition

DAVID NOVAK

WITH CHRISTA BOURG

PORTFOLIO / PENGUIN

An imprint of Penguin Random House LLC
375 Hudson Street
New York, New York 10014

Library of Congress Cataloging-in-Publication Data Available
ISBN: 9780399562068
ISBN (e-book): 9780399562082

Printed in the United States of America
1   3   5   7   9   10   8   6   4   2

Book design by Cassandra Garruzzo

This book is dedicated to attacking the recognition deficit that exists in our world today. To all the people out there who are doing great things and deserve to be recognized for it, this story is for you.

Contents

Introduction

O Great One!: The Story

OGO—short for O Great One—is the name my grandkids have called me ever since they could talk. It may sound over the top to some, but it came about because when my daughter was pregnant with her first child, I didn't want to be called grandpa, poppy, or any of the usual names. I wanted something a bit more fun and different. How OGO finally came to me is something I will tell in the coming story, but over the years, people always laughed when they heard the name. It was also easy for my grandkids to say, so it stuck.

Since then, OGO has become much, much more than just a nickname my family calls me. It has come to represent something I've practiced and encouraged throughout my entire life: the awesome power of recognition.

O Great One! is a story about that powerful force. It centers on a guy named Jeff Johnson, who becomes CEO of the Happy Face Toy Company, an organization that's in dire shape when he arrives. Because he's new to the job, and even new to the industry, he's left scrambling and not sure what to do about the company's ever-sinking sales. That is, until a surprise gift from his grandson helps him discover that in his organization, recognition has been the missing ingredient that will turn things around—for him, for his team, and for Happy Face Toys as a whole.

I wanted to tell this story because I've seen how impactful recognition can be. I've also witnessed how devastating it can be when it's absent from the life of an individual, a team, and even a large organization. Often people think of recognition as the kind of fluffy feel-good stuff that businesses talk about to try to make their employees happy. But if used right, it does a whole lot more than that. Simply put: if you give people the recognition they've *earned,* if you show *genuine* appreciation and acknowledge the unique things people have to offer, then you will drive real results. And at the same time, you will lift the spirits of everyone involved. It really does feel good to receive recognition, and it feels every bit as good to give it—often even better.

Considering that recognition can have such a hugely positive effect, it's amazing to me that it's still vastly underused in business, and also in life. I think that's a crime. As you'll see in this story, making use of recognition is not hard, it's not expensive, and you don't need an MBA or even a position of authority to do it.

I know this is true because I've seen it in action as my team and I built Yum! Brands into one of the world's largest restaurant companies. It operates in 125 countries and employs nearly 1.5 million people. So I've not only seen recognition work, I've also seen it work on a grand scale with people from different walks of life all around the world. In fact, the story you are about to read is based on real-world experiences I've had throughout my career as the leader of this mammoth organization.

This story comes from my personal experience, but that doesn't mean you have to be the leader of a big company to reap the benefits. Recognition works for the leader of a small team just as well as it does for the chairman of a large enterprise. It works for an individual who isn't in a leadership position at all. It works outside of business for parents, teachers, community groups, sports teams, and everyone else. The important thing to understand about recognition is that it's simply good for people—*all people*—no matter who they are, what they do, or where they come from.

If there's one message I hope you will take away from this book it's that no matter who you are or what you do, *you* have the power to use recognition to make a difference in people's lives each and every day. You have the power to show people that someone is watching, that someone cares, and that what they do really matters. You have the power to help individuals, teams, and organizations reach their potential. Whether you're trying to affect the bottom line of a Fortune 500 company or the quality of life of your children, the prescription is the same. If you use recognition on a regular basis, you can inspire people to do great things. And the personal satisfaction you'll receive as a result, when you see others reach their full potential with your help . . . well, that's when the real magic kicks in.

O Great One! is for anyone who wants to motivate people, get results, and feed the soul. And really, who wouldn't want to do all that? Especially because it all comes down to something that's relatively simple to implement and use.

As far as I'm concerned, the only real question is: *Why aren't people using recognition more?*

PART I

The Bob Problem

Chapter 1

Jeff Johnson was uneasy as he drove down an unfamiliar road on the outskirts of Cleveland. He had been there before, but not for many years, and the area had changed. What used to be a remote location was now a busy commercial district filled with office buildings, restaurants, and even a Starbucks on the corner. In the distance he could see his destination: a sprawling complex of squat, gray buildings housing production facilities for the Happy Face Toy Company.

It had been only one month since Jeff was appointed CEO of Happy Face Toys. It wasn't a role he'd expected to play at this point in his life, but circumstances had conspired to make it happen. Happy Face Toys was more than just a business to Jeff; it was the family business, his family's legacy. Currently that business was in real trouble, and he was the only Johnson in a position to do something about it.

Happy Face Toys was started in 1953 by Jeff's grandfather, who had worked tirelessly to grow it from a small factory making just one product into an international toy manufacturer. Jeff's father had taken over in the late 1980s, after his grandfather's retirement, and expanded it even further, making it the industry leader for many years. During high school and college, Jeff spent summers working in the company mail room, but after graduating, he chose to forge his own career path. He moved to California to join a software company. He'd done well in the technology sector and always assumed he'd finish out his career there, never imagining he would end up back in the family business. But the death of his father a few months before had forced his hand.

When Jeff's father died, the company was faltering, and there was no clear successor to take his place. Losing his father was hard enough. Jeff couldn't stand to see Happy Face fail as well, and he didn't trust anyone to care as much as he did about its success. So when he started hearing rumors that the board of directors was thinking about selling the business, he made a choice. He quit his job in California and moved to Chicago, where the company had its headquarters, ready to follow in his father's footsteps as CEO of the family business.

Jeff believed in his heart that it was the right thing to do, but it still hadn't been an easy decision. He and his wife had lived in California for more than twenty years. Their

4

daughter had been raised there and still lived nearby with her own family. Leaving them behind was tough on everyone. Jeff was really hoping the sacrifice would be worth it. Unfortunately, not everyone at Happy Face was thrilled with the idea of his taking over.

Happy Face Toys had been on a slow decline for nearly a decade. Steadily increasing competition from overseas and a lack of innovative new products were the reasons most commonly cited within the company. Even before Jeff's father passed away, the board of directors had been talking about making big changes, including bringing in fresh talent. The company clearly had considerable financial problems, but Jeff wasn't so sure the board had the right vision for how to address them. And because he now owned 49 percent of the company's stock—thanks to an inheritance from his father—they had to take him seriously.

Even still, when he proposed himself as his father's successor, the board wasn't convinced that Jeff, with his lack of experience in the toy industry, was the right choice. In a moment of boldness or desperation (he wasn't sure which), Jeff presented the board with a challenge: "Give me one year. If I can't turn things around and get this company back on track in that time, then fire me and bring in whoever you want. I won't fight you."

So they gave him the job. The problem was that Jeff had no idea how he was going to keep that job.

The Cleveland plant he was now driving toward was where Happy Face Toys had first started more than sixty years before, and it had continued to be the company's headquarters and sole manufacturing plant for many years after that. Then the business took off and things changed. As Happy Face grew into an international brand, most of the business functions were moved to a large office building in Chicago, and newer, larger, state-of-the-art facilities were built in China and Mexico, where the vast majority of their products were now made. During that time the Cleveland plant had gradually shrunk to become mostly a distribution hub for its U.S. business. Throughout all the changes, however, the plant had remained open. In fact, it still manufactured the first big product that Happy Face ever launched: Crazy Paste, a brightly colored molding clay that every kid in America had played with in the 1950s and 1960s. Crazy Paste wasn't nearly as popular as it once had been, but it still had a nostalgic value in the marketplace.

Jeff had a difficult decision to make as the new CEO. The Cleveland plant had been struggling for years, and the board of directors thought it was high time to shut it down. Jeff had nearly agreed—the numbers spoke for themselves—but at the last minute he decided to wait. If he was going to shutter a piece of company history, a piece of his family's legacy, and cause hundreds of people to lose their jobs, the least he could do was visit the place first.

It was his first big decision as CEO and it wasn't a popular one. In fact, Jeff had already heard rumbles that many of the company's senior leaders thought it was a crazy first move and a big waste of time. After all, the failure of the Cleveland plant was just the tip of the iceberg, and there were so many more problems to be solved to get Happy Face back on track. As a new leader, Jeff didn't want to give the impression that he had trouble making hard decisions, but his instincts told him this was what he needed to do. He didn't have high expectations for his visit, but he hoped he might get some sense of how things had gone so terribly wrong. And if he did end up closing the plant, at least he could do it with a clean conscience, knowing he'd given the matter a thorough review.

As he pulled into the parking lot of the production plant, with its badly chipped paint and ancient sign reading **HAP Y ACE TO S!**, he couldn't help but wonder whether the doubters were right, whether he was indeed making a colossal mistake.

Chapter 2

As Jeff swung open the large front doors of the Happy Face plant, he was surprised to find a silent, empty room. There was no reception desk, no one there to greet him, not even a sign to point him in the direction of the plant manager. This was nothing like the place he remembered visiting when he was young, with its shiny floors, the company's name in polished gold letters displayed proudly on the wall, and a receptionist who always had a smile on her face and a bowl of candy on her desk that he couldn't wait to dig into. When he was a kid, Jeff thought this was the happiest place on earth. Clearly, that wasn't the case anymore.

This isn't a good sign, he said to himself. He started to pull out his cell phone to call his assistant back in Chicago. She would find someone at the plant to come out and get him.

On second thought, Jeff put his phone back in his pocket.

Maybe it was better this way. It would give him a chance to see how things really worked without the show people typically put on for the CEO.

With that in mind, Jeff started to wander down a hallway. The first thing he saw was a trophy case that reminded him of one at his high school. Way back when, Jeff had played on the basketball team, and they had gone all the way to the state championships. He hadn't been a star player, but he'd loved being part of that team, so the trophy case brought back fond memories. He smiled as he leaned forward to take a closer look.

Inside the case was a large plaque that read EMPLOYEE OF THE MONTH. The plaque was inscribed with the names of dozens of employees who had earned the honor over the years.

That's a nice thing to have on such prominent display, he thought. But then he frowned and peered a little closer. He looked at the last name inscribed on the plaque. It read, "Carmen Ruiz, October 2006."

"That can't be the last time they had an Employee of the Month around here," Jeff said aloud to no one in particular. Could it really be that no one had won the honor in nearly a decade? It seemed impossible. It also seemed like yet another bad sign, another indication that the board of directors had been right in wanting to close the plant. If no one had been given the title of Employee of the

Month in all that time, then maybe the plant's best days really were behind it.

There was a part of Jeff that was tempted to turn around and head back to Chicago right then and there, to go back home and tell the board he agreed with them. But something in his gut told him to press on.

He continued down the hallway. As he got closer to a pair of double doors at the end of the hall, he could hear the sound of raised voices in the distance. Intent on following the noise, he pushed open the doors and found himself in a massive warehouse lined with boxes from floor to ceiling. At the other end of the warehouse was a truck bay, next to which two men were having an argument. Their voices echoed in the cavernous space so that even though Jeff was quite a distance away, he could make out every word of their conversation.

"Why aren't your guys loading up those trucks?" the first man was shouting.

"My guys *are* loading the trucks. They're just on break right now, that's all," the second guy answered.

"I was just out there, and there's barely anything on those trucks. If that's the fastest you can go, then we have a problem," the first guy threatened.

"We have a problem all right, but it's not because of my guys," the second guy shot back. "My guys could load those trucks up in no time, but it still wouldn't matter.

The trucks would still be sitting out there because they've got no drivers."

"What do you mean they've got no drivers?"

"Just what I said. There's no one to drive those trucks off this lot."

"Have you called Sam about that?"

"No."

"Why not?"

"Because it's my job to make sure the trucks get loaded. My guys are here, and they're doing their jobs. The drivers are not my responsibility. Have *you* talked to Sam about why there are no drivers here?"

"Why would I have talked to Sam? I didn't even know there was a problem until just now. Where is Sam, anyway?"

"How would I know? He works for you, doesn't he?"

Jeff couldn't believe what he was hearing. No wonder this place was falling apart.

"Excuse me!" The two men abruptly stopped talking and looked around, not sure where the voice was coming from.

"Excuse me!" Jeff said again from the other end of the warehouse, waving a hand in the air. The men had spotted him now, and Jeff started crossing the floor toward them.

"Who are you?" the first man grunted when Jeff was about halfway to them. He hadn't recognized Jeff. Not yet.

Jeff wasn't interested in starting off this conversation

with more yelling and screaming, so he simply kept walking in their direction. He would answer the man when they were face to face.

As it turned out, he didn't have to answer. As Jeff made his way closer, the first man's face abruptly changed, first to a look of shocked surprise, then embarrassment, and then it fell. He had clearly recognized the new CEO of the Happy Face Toy Company, and he didn't appear happy to see him.

"I'm Jeff Johnson," Jeff said when he finally reached the two men. He was careful to keep both his voice and his expression as neutral as possible, which took some effort because he was pretty ticked off about what he had seen and heard so far during his visit to Cleveland.

"Sir, we . . . we weren't expecting you until this afternoon," the first man stammered.

"I arrived early," Jeff said simply. Then he stuck out his hand. "And your name is?"

"Oh, it's Doug. Doug Yearwood. Plant manager. And this is our loading dock supervisor . . ."

"Gabriel," the second man said, moving forward to shake Jeff's hand.

The air was thick with tension, but Jeff wanted to move past the awkwardness as quickly as possible and get down to business.

In order to diffuse things, he smiled and said, "It's

nice to meet you both. I've been looking forward to my visit here. It's my first time in Cleveland in many years. I used to visit my grandfather here as a child, but that was a very long time ago."

With that, the two men relaxed a bit. Jeff thought he even heard a sigh of relief escape from Doug.

"Sir," Doug said, recovering some of his composure, "why don't we continue our conversation back in my office. We planned to start off your visit today by showing you a video that talks about the history of this plant. Like I said, we weren't expecting you until this afternoon, but I'm sure if we can find our office manager, Carmen, she'll cue it up for you. And then I thought I'd take you on a tour of the facility . . ."

"Thanks, Doug. I appreciate the effort, but I think I'd rather start off a bit differently. I'd like to meet the people who work here."

"Oh, OK," Doug said, trying to sound happy about the change of plans. "I could take you on that tour now and introduce you to some of our supervisors."

"Thanks again, Doug, but when I said I wanted to meet people, I meant I wanted to meet *all* the people who work here. Not just the managers and supervisors."

"OK . . ." Doug replied.

"In fact, I'd like you to call a meeting. Is there any place big enough for everyone to gather in at once?"

"Well, I'm not sure . . ." Doug said.

"Everyone could fit here in the warehouse," Gabriel piped up.

"Great!" Jeff said.

"And we've got some folding chairs in storage we could bring in if you want," Gabriel added.

"Even better," Jeff said.

"But sir," Doug said worriedly. "We've got several production lines going, trucks to load, all sorts of things to get done. If we have *everyone* at the meeting, we'll basically have to shut down the plant for the rest of the day."

"That's the plan," Jeff said. "How long will it take you to set everything up in here, Gabriel?"

"If I pull my guys off what they're doing right now, maybe an hour?" Gabriel replied.

"Perfect. And Doug, how long will it take you to get word to everyone about the meeting?"

"Well, some of the drivers are already out for the day. I'll have to call them back. And some of the people in the office might not be at their desks . . ."

"What's the quickest you can make it happen?" Jeff asked.

"Maybe two hours?" Doug replied.

"Great! Then let's set the meeting for right after lunch. And plan to shut down production for the rest of the day."

"But sir." Doug was looking very uneasy about all of

this. Gabriel, meanwhile, was enjoying his boss's look of discomfort.

"Yes?" said Jeff, still trying to keep his voice calm even though he really just wanted Doug to do what he'd asked.

"Well. . . . I guess I was just wondering . . ."

"Wondering what?" Jeff asked.

"I guess I was wondering, are you sure about all this?"

"I'm absolutely sure," Jeff said. "I'll see you both again right after lunch."

Chapter 3

Once the meeting was set, Jeff headed back to his car, not because he had anywhere to go, but because he needed to take a deep breath and calm down.

As soon as he reached his car, he checked his messages and then called his assistant, Marjorie, back in Chicago.

"Anything important going on?" he asked her.

"Just the same old stuff. How's it going there?" she asked.

"It's . . . interesting," Jeff responded, not sure what to say about what he'd seen so far. "It's really too soon to tell."

"I think people are wondering why you bothered to go to Cleveland at all," Marjorie said carefully.

"What do you mean?" Jeff asked. He knew what she meant, but he wanted to know what she'd heard.

"I overheard Anna this morning telling some people that closing the Cleveland plant was all but a done deal.

She said you must have gone out there just to say good-bye to your granddad's old stomping ground."

"She said that, did she," Jeff sighed. Anna was their chief information officer (CIO), and she had been up front from the beginning that she agreed with the board about closing down the plant. Jeff got the feeling she also agreed with the board about the idea of bringing in someone from outside the family, someone who at least had some consumer product experience, to head the company. He could tell already it was going to take some serious convincing to get Anna on his side and to buy into his vision for the company. But first things first: he had to figure out what that vision was. And that started with deciding what to do about the plant in Cleveland.

"Well, thanks for letting me know," Jeff said, deciding to let it go for now. "I've got a meeting with the entire plant this afternoon, so I'll have my phone off. But I'll check in with you at the end of the day."

"OK, good luck," Marjorie said, trying to sound upbeat.

"Thanks. I think I'll need it," Jeff said.

He hung up the phone and just sat there for a while. *What am I doing?* he wondered. *Why don't I just do what everyone back in Chicago wants me to do and close this place down? After all, they know a lot more about the business than I do. A month ago, I was an executive at a software company, which is a far cry from making toys. And from what I've seen and heard so far in Cleveland, it doesn't seem like the people here care all that much about making this place succeed. So why should I?*

Then Jeff thought about what it had felt like to look into that trophy case. Nearly ten years in which no employees had been publicly acknowledged for their work. Nearly ten years since anyone had been acknowledged as Employee of the Month. He stared up at the battered **HAP Y ACE TO S!** sign on the front of the building. It looked as if it had been in bad shape for quite some time, and yet no one had bothered to fix it.

Something was very wrong with this picture. The company's leadership clearly hadn't done much to show its employees in Cleveland that it cared about them. At least not recently. And if the company didn't care about them, why should they care about the company?

Besides, he knew that many of these people had worked for his dad. Some of them had even been around long enough to have worked for his grandfather. Before making such a big and final decision about closing the place down, he wanted to get to the bottom of why things were the way they were. He figured he owed these people at least that much. And he could start by asking them a simple question: What's happened to this place? Chances were they had some thoughts, especially those who had seen the once thriving plant falter and erode to the state it was in

18

today. Jeff's mind was made up. During the meeting, that's exactly what he would do. He would ask his employees that question and then sit back and listen to what they had to say.

This won't be so hard, he thought. He had no idea what was in store for him that afternoon.

Chapter 4

When Jeff walked into the warehouse for the second time that day, the atmosphere was very different. The sprawling space was packed with people sitting in chairs or standing in groups, but the room was much quieter than it had been before. No one was yelling or arguing now. In fact, it was eerily quiet.

As Jeff stood by the doorway surveying the scene, Gabriel and Doug approached him.

"Sir, we set up a kind of platform for you up front there," Gabriel said, motioning to what looked like the top of a shipping crate. "That way the people in back can see you better."

"And we managed to get everyone here," Doug chimed in. "Everyone who is working today, at least."

"I think everyone's really interested to hear what you have to say," Gabriel added.

Jeff wondered if that were true. As he looked out over

the crowd, he saw a lot of disinterested-looking faces. But he had an important question to ask these people, and nothing was going to stop him from asking it. So he thanked Doug and Gabriel, took a deep breath, and stepped onto the makeshift platform.

"Let me start by introducing myself," Jeff called out. "Can everyone hear me in the back?"

No one answered, but he saw a few heads nod back there and figured that was enough to continue.

"My name is Jeff Johnson, and as you probably know, I'm the new CEO of Happy Face Toys. Many of you probably knew my father, who was CEO before me. Some of you, I think, even knew my grandfather, who was CEO before that and the founder of this great company." Jeff had been hoping for a few more head nods, maybe even some reassuring smiles, but all he saw were stony expressions.

"When my grandfather started this company sixty years ago, his mission was 'to put a smile on every child's face.' Thanks to the efforts of the people in this room and many more around the world, we've come a long way toward achieving that mission. This facility produced one of the most popular, iconic toys the industry has ever seen. Since then, we've grown our operations to make hundreds of products and expanded our reach to children around the globe. Happy Face Toys is a brand that's known around the world. And it all started right here . . ."

Jeff paused then because he was about to shift his tone. That was the company's past. Now it was time to talk about the present. And the present wasn't nearly as happy a story.

"The past few years, however, have been tough," Jeff continued, choosing his words carefully. "The company has gone through a lot of changes and the industry has gone through a lot of changes as well. Frankly, we aren't as successful as we used to be . . ."

Jeff paused again, unsure of whether he should say what he wanted to say next. He didn't want to scare anyone, and he didn't want to come across as a downer. But he also figured there was no use sugarcoating things. Back at headquarters, people were talking about closing this place down as if it were a done deal. While he didn't want to go that far, he did want everyone in this room to understand that the situation was dire.

"In fact, we've been losing ground for quite some time now. And we're at a critical juncture. Either we work together to turn this company around, or some of us might not have our jobs for much longer. And that includes me. I promised the board I would get this company back on track within a year. If I don't, they'll fire me. Simple as that."

That got their attention. Quiet murmurs spread through the crowd. Jeff waited for them to die down before continuing.

"I'm here today to ask for your help. I want to know what you think our problems are. Of course I don't expect you to answer for what's gone wrong with the entire company, but many of the problems we face as an organization are the same problems you face right here in this plant. Because I'm new to my position, and you're the ones who come here to work every day, I'm asking you: What's gone wrong? What's not working and why? How could we do better?"

Jeff paused again and looked out over the crowd. He'd been hoping people would just start chiming in, but in truth, most of them looked a little uncomfortable. So he added, "I want you to know that this isn't some kind of test. And it isn't a critique. I'm really just here to listen. I want to know what *you* think about how things are working around here."

The big question, Jeff knew, was whether they believed he really wanted to hear what they had to say.

Jeff stared out at the crowd, hoping they could sense the sincerity behind his question. And they stared silently back at him. His natural tendency was to speak up when things got quiet, to fill the silence and get the ball rolling, but he didn't want to do that now. He was asking a lot of them, and they deserved a minute to gather their thoughts. He wanted them to be comfortable, and he was willing to give them all the time they needed. So as hard as it was for him, he kept his mouth shut. Instead, he just stood there on the makeshift stage with what he hoped was a welcoming smile on his face.

After a few more moments, he felt his smile starting to crack at the edges. He was wondering how much longer he could stand the awkwardness when, finally, he heard a familiar voice coming from the edge of the group.

"Um, sir?"

Jeff turned to see Gabriel raising his hand.

"Yes, Gabriel. You have something to say?"

"Yeah, well. I don't quite know how to say it, but . . . Well, you obviously heard Doug and me talking this morning about the trucks."

"I did," Jeff answered, careful not to sound judgmental.

"Well, we were talking about a problem we've been having for quite some time. We get the trucks loaded with product, but then there's no one to drive them."

"So then . . ." Jeff said. This seemed like a problem that should be easy to solve. "Why don't you get more drivers in here?"

"Well, that's the thing. It used to be that we could just hire drivers when we needed them, but now we have to go through headquarters to get approval and it takes forever."

"Yeah," someone standing near Gabriel added. "I used to be able to just call up some guys and get them in here within a day. Now it takes ten times as long to go through corporate's process for hiring just one measly part-time guy. I have to fill out all this paperwork, send it to head-quarters, and then call and call over there to get approval. By the time I do, it's just too darn late!"

"What's your name?"

"I'm Sam. I'm in charge of the drivers and have been for twenty years. The thing is, we never had this problem before. Not until you guys instituted the new hiring process last year. That process might work for you all back in Chicago, where you only hire long-term employees, but here our needs change all the time. And that process has just been a disaster for us. But if I don't follow it, then my drivers don't get paid."

"I see," Jeff said. "That does sound like a real problem. Have you talked to human resources about it?"

"I've tried," Sam sighed. "And tried. And tried."

"Well, then, it sounds as if they don't fully understand how important it is. When I get back to Chicago, I'm going to talk to HR right away. I'm going to make sure they understand that fixing this is a top priority and have someone call you to work it out."

"That would be great," Sam said with a note of skepticism.

"I'm writing this down to make sure I don't forget," Jeff said, pulling a piece of paper and a pen out of his breast pocket. "And Sam . . ."

"Yes?"

"If no one has called you and the problem isn't on its way to being fixed within a week, I want you to call me directly."

"Really?"

"Yes. I'll give you my direct line before I leave."

Suddenly, a wave of murmurs swept through the crowd, picking up steam as it went. Jeff could tell that he was finally starting to get their attention.

"So what else?" he asked. At least a dozen hands shot up.

Chapter 5

For the next two hours, Jeff stood up on his platform and fielded questions and complaints of all kinds.

The office manager, Carmen, wanted to know why they didn't have family picnics anymore. For years the company had sponsored an annual picnic that everyone attended along with their families. "We don't do anything fun like that anymore," she told him. "Nothing to make us feel like we're connected and part of a team."

Julie, one of the engineers from the group that produced Crazy Paste, wanted to know if they were ever going to make anything new and different. "It's not that I don't love Crazy Paste," she said. "It's just that we've sent out proposal after proposal about ways to extend the product line with new products we could make right here using the equipment we already have."

"And what's been the response?" Jeff asked. He hadn't heard about any new proposals.

"That's just it," Julie replied. "There hasn't been a response. It's like sending ideas into a black hole. They just disappear like they never even existed in the first place. Sometimes I think that Chicago has forgotten all about us."

Jeff was alarmed by how many people in the crowd seemed to agree with that sentiment. More hands shot up from people wanting to discuss everything from overtime pay to sprucing up the facility to overhauling processes in one department after another. Employees from the front office blamed the production group when questions were raised about how long it took to get product out the door. Production, in turn, pointed the finger at the people in operations, who were in charge of packing and shipping. Operations then started criticizing the front office again. Jeff was starting to think the conversation was focusing too much on the negatives. To change things up a bit, he asked what he thought was a pretty straightforward question about something they did well.

"This plant has a great track record when it comes to creating merchandising displays to showcase our products for our retail customers. What do you think about our efforts today?"

Right away, someone spoke up, "Bob is the expert in that area. He can tell you how it's done."

Someone else added, "Bob taught me more about merchandising in one day than I'd learned in two years on the job."

"Yup, he's the one who always comes up with the most innovative new ideas," yet another voice added. "And he knows how to see those ideas through to make sure they're done right."

"Bob's the best there is. Everyone here knows that."

Heads started nodding in agreement around the room. Jeff was amazed. It appeared *everyone* in the room actually agreed on something. When it came to merchandising, they all believed that Bob was a star.

"So," Jeff said smiling, pleased to have finally stumbled upon something positive to talk about, "which one of you is this infamous Bob?"

Several people pointed toward a man in his sixties, sitting in a chair off to the left. Jeff looked over at Bob, thinking he must be thrilled by all this praise, but when he saw Bob, his smile disappeared.

Bob was slumped down in his chair, staring at his hands. When Jeff looked closer, he could see tears running down Bob's face. And they didn't appear to be tears of joy either. In fact, Bob looked downright dismayed.

"Bob," Jeff said carefully, "there are so many people here heaping praise on you, but you're clearly upset. What's wrong?"

Bob took a deep breath before he looked up and met Jeff's gaze. Then he spoke so quietly that Jeff had to strain to hear him.

"I've been with this company for forty-seven years and I'm going to be retiring in two weeks," Bob told him. "In all that time, I never knew anyone felt this way about me."

Jeff was stunned. All the momentum that had been building in the room suddenly fell flat as everyone stared at Bob. Jeff gathered himself together and walked over to him. He bent down and put his arm around Bob's shoulder before saying quietly to him, "Bob, everyone here obviously thinks the world of you. I'm sorry no one has said it to you before, but I think you should be really, really proud."

Chapter 6

After what happened with Bob, Jeff felt as if he'd pushed the people of Cleveland far enough. He returned to the stage just long enough to thank everyone for their candor and to promise he would take everything he'd heard back to Chicago and then return in a few weeks with real answers.

As the meeting broke up, Jeff decided to hang around for a while in case anyone else wanted to talk. A few people approached him to offer their thoughts, and some even thanked him for taking the time to listen. As Jeff chatted with the last of the group, he noticed how many people had gone over and given Bob a pat on the back. That seemed to have really bucked him up, which Jeff was relieved to see.

After the last of the crowd had dispersed, Jeff walked back to the parking lot. As he did so, he couldn't help wondering if what he'd just experienced should be considered a success or a failure. He felt as if he'd broken through and started a productive dialogue with the people at the plant. He'd also learned a lot about what wasn't working and why, not just in Cleveland but in the company as a whole. And most important, he'd discovered something he hadn't been so sure of earlier that morning: the people in Cleveland really did care about the success of the company.

At the same time, he kept thinking about Bob. It was such a shame that Bob had never felt appreciated for his excellent work and obvious talent. It was a huge missed opportunity for the business too. More people could have learned from him and benefited from his expertise. He was obviously great at what he did, but who knows how much better he could have been in a workplace that appreciated and cultivated his talents. What's more, Jeff was certain that if someone as good as Bob felt overlooked and undervalued, then surely others did too.

The same question kept playing over and over in his head: *How will we ever succeed in this organization if this is how our people feel?*

Jeff was starting to think the answer to this question was key to the company's future success. It was clear to him that none of their problems, even beyond the ones discussed that day, could be entirely fixed if they didn't first fix their "Bob problem."

As Jeff drove away from the plant, he felt deflated. He was headed back to Chicago that evening so he could celebrate his birthday. His daughter and her family had come in from California for the weekend just for the occasion, and he knew there would be lots of questions about how things were going at work. Questions that he didn't have good answers to. He didn't want to have to tell his family that the company had big problems. He didn't want to have to admit that he had no idea how to fix those problems. And most of all, he didn't want to have to say that disrupting their lives and moving halfway across the country to run the family business may have been a huge mistake.

Chapter 7

"OGO!" Jeff's grandson, Nick, called out as soon as Jeff walked through the front door. The gray cloud around Jeff immediately lifted as his grandson made a beeline for him and wrapped his arms around Jeff's knees.

OGO was the name Nick had called Jeff ever since he could talk. Eight years earlier, when his daughter, Allison, had gotten pregnant, Jeff decided that at the age of fifty-two, he was far too young to be called grandpa, poppy, or any of the other traditional names, so he started thinking about something that might suit him better.

His late father-in-law had been Great Jack to his daughter, which Jeff had always liked, and he wanted something equally catchy and fun for himself. His first thought was to go by Great Jeff, but somehow that didn't have the same ring to it. He considered a few other ideas, but nothing sounded quite right. And then it came to him out of the blue.

He tried not to smile as he announced his spin on Great Jack to his wife and daughter one evening. "I've decided the grandkids should call me OGO."

His wife Sarah burst out laughing. "OGO, what's that?"

"It stands for O Great One," Jeff responded in all sincerity, "and they can call me OGO for short!" His family cracked up.

Over the years, every time Jeff told someone about the name he'd come up with, they couldn't help but laugh. And it was easy for young kids to say, so the nickname stuck. In his grandson's eyes, Jeff had always been his OGO.

Jeff reached down to grab Nick's hand, and together they walked into the kitchen to join the rest of the family. Soon Jeff was kicking himself for worrying about the evening. It was the first time the whole family had been together since he and his wife had left California, and Jeff realized this was exactly what he needed to clear his head and focus on the positive for a while. When his son-in-law asked him about work, he simply said, "We're still figuring out the transition. It's going to take some time." Everyone accepted that answer and moved on to other topics.

After a lively dinner, Sarah announced that it was time for presents.

"Oh no, you shouldn't have," Jeff protested. "You all came here to see me. What more could I want?"

"Too late now," Sarah said. "They're already wrapped and waiting for you in the living room. Besides, Nick and Allison have something special for you."

Jeff looked over at his grandson, who flashed him a shy smile. "I'm gonna save ours for last," Nick said.

After Jeff had opened most of his presents and eaten far too much birthday cake, Allison looked at Nick and asked gently, "How about now?"

Nick ran out of the room to fetch his present. Allison turned to Jeff and said, "We've been working on this all day, and Nick's been so excited about giving it to you." Everyone was grinning with anticipation. Jeff knew it was going to be something out of the ordinary, but he had no idea what the present might be.

When Nick returned, he was holding something behind his back. He walked straight up to his grandfather and dropped it in his lap. "For you!" he shouted with pride.

Jeff looked down and saw an old glass mason jar. On the front was a big red sticker with the word "OGO" printed on it in black capital letters.

"What is it?" Jeff asked.

"You have to open it," Sarah prompted.

Jeff unscrewed the lid. Inside he saw what looked like ribbons of construction paper in all different colors. He pulled one out and looked at it. Someone had written a message on it that read, "O Great One, you're great because . . ." Then Jeff turned it over. On the back, it said, "I love it when you take me to the park."

Jeff chuckled at that and then reached in and pulled out another piece of paper.

"O Great One, you're great because . . . You always know how to make me laugh."

Then another.

"O Great One, you're great because . . . On my wedding day you gave a toast that everyone still talks about to this day."

And another.

"O Great One, you're great because . . . You were there when I needed you the most."

Jeff stopped pulling out pieces of paper because his eyes had started filling with tears.

"What is this?" Jeff asked, looking around the room at his family.

"Well, we know you already have practically everything you could ever want," Allison explained, "so we figured that in addition to the usual odds and ends, we would give you something that showed you much we've missed you and how special you are to us. It was Nick's idea to make the OGO jar."

"This is the best present I've ever gotten," Jeff said quietly. "Thank you, all of you."

Nick was beaming at him, so Jeff reached over and gave his grandson a big bear hug.

As the evening came to a close, Jeff realized the time with his family and their unusual gift had really turned his day around. Little did he know just how much power was packed inside that simple glass jar.

👑 👑 👑

Later that night, after everyone had gone to bed, Jeff took his OGO jar into his study. The gift had taken him by surprise. He was used to getting presents from his family, but they usually consisted of books, or golf balls, or a new sweater. He had never received anything quite like this before. Opening it, especially in front of his whole family, had been quite an emotional experience.

Jeff sat down at his desk and finished reading the messages inside his OGO jar. As he read through them, he suddenly felt better about the move than he had before. They were a tight-knit family, and he knew they would stay that way no matter where any of them lived.

After Jeff had read the last message, he folded up all the pieces of paper, returned them carefully to the jar, and screwed on the lid. He stood up and cleared a space on the shelf next to his desk. There he gave his OGO jar a place of pride next to the awards he had received over the years for his work and community service.

He sat back down at his desk and gazed up at the shelf. It was amazing to him to think he'd been feeling so down just a few hours earlier, and now he couldn't imagine feeling any better. There certainly was something very powerful about feeling appreciated for who you are and what you do.

Jeff thought about Bob then and wondered how things might have been different if someone had just found a way to thank him for all that he'd done. He also thought about the company's mission "to put a smile on every child's face." How were they ever going to make their customers happy if they couldn't make their own people happy first?

As Jeff sat there replaying the day's events in his head, he suddenly knew what he needed to do. About the plant and whether to close it down. About the board and his team in Chicago. About the entire company and how to fix what was broken.

He realized that he wouldn't have a snowball's chance of turning the company around if he didn't make firing up their people his top priority. He now had a great idea for how to do that and how to grow Happy Toys from that day forward. For the first time since he had packed up his life to move to Chicago, Jeff believed he was on the right track.

Now he just had to persuade everyone else to go along with him.

PART II

The OGO Answer

Chapter 8

The following Monday morning, Jeff got up and looked in the mirror. He had barely slept the night before because his mind had been racing about all the things he wanted to accomplish during his team meeting that day. He knew he was about to shake things up at the Happy Face Toy Company, and he knew he'd be challenged because of it. Change always made people uncomfortable, but he was convinced that big change was exactly what they needed. As he gazed at his reflection, he reminded himself that he would really have to bring his A game today if he was to have any hope of getting his team to embrace the kind of changes he planned to propose.

Like most people, Jeff wasn't comfortable with conflict, so he was apprehensive about how the meeting would go. But he was also eager to share his new vision for the company. He walked into his Chicago office that morning with his OGO jar proudly tucked under his arm and greeted his assistant with a big smile.

"Good morning, Marjorie!"

"Good morning," Marjorie replied, sounding more than a little surprised. "You're in a good mood. After your end-of-the-day report on Friday, I wasn't sure what we were in for this morning."

"It's a new beginning," Jeff said. Before she could ask what he meant, he continued, "Is everything ready for the team meeting this morning?"

"All set. Everyone will be in the conference room in half an hour."

"Great, and thanks. I really appreciate all your efforts."

"Well, of course," Marjorie said with a little laugh. "I guess you must have had a really good weekend with your family."

"I did indeed, Marjorie," Jeff said before disappearing into his office.

For the next thirty minutes Jeff sat at his desk reviewing what he wanted to say to his executive team. He felt confident about his new vision for Happy Face Toys, but less so about how the team would react to it. He knew his vision wouldn't work if he couldn't get every one of them on board, so this meeting was a crucial first step. He expected some pushback from at least one or two members of the group, but because he was new to his position, there were several people who were still question marks to him. He wasn't so sure what they would think about the changes he wanted to make.

Jeff mentally scrolled through his team roster, trying to anticipate how each person would react.

First, there was Anna, the imperious CIO from whom Jeff had already encountered some tension. Anna had been a Rhodes scholar and a top athlete in college, and she had the confidence to match. She had strong ideas, which was a good thing, but she also came across as someone who believed she already had all the answers. During team meetings, he'd noticed that she was often quick to point out others' mistakes or holes in their thinking, but he'd never seen her admit to such things herself. Jeff didn't entirely blame her for this. He'd encountered many executives over the years who believed that being in a leadership position meant you had to be right all the time. Anna had probably been taught to lead this way by those who'd come before her, but it was an old way of thinking and one that wasn't going to work for the new Happy Face Toy Company. Jeff didn't want to write her off too soon, but he was concerned that she wasn't the kind of leader who wanted to reexamine the way she did things.

Next, there was Adam, their chief legal officer and the most experienced member of the team. He'd been with the company for more than a decade, and he'd had an impressive career in manufacturing even before that. So far, Jeff hadn't had much chance to interact with him personally, but he had noticed that Adam was highly logical and someone other people deferred to. When Adam spoke during team meetings, he used a deep baritone voice that conveyed absolute authority. As a result, unfortunately, conversation too often came to an abrupt halt. People simply took him at his word, and it appeared that no one wanted to question him or ask him for more details, let alone disagree with him. Jeff suspected this was mostly a communication problem and that Adam didn't realize the effect he was having on people. After all, Jeff was pretty sure no one had ever told him. Jeff knew that that unhappy job might fall to him one day soon, but he wasn't too worried about it. He'd had to confront people about such things before, and it usually turned out fine once everyone got past their initial discomfort.

By contrast, Dan, their head of operations and human resources and the newest member of the team besides Jeff, was an amiable guy. He had been the first one to seek out Jeff to welcome him to Chicago. Jeff had spoken to him frequently since then and always enjoyed it when they ran into each other in the hallway. But he'd also noticed something peculiar about their conversations: Dan had a way of steering the topic away from business and toward a more personal topic. He talked often about his family, his love of scuba diving, his dream of one day sailing around the world, but very little about what he was working on or what his current challenges were. Jeff liked him and it appeared that every-one else did too, even Adam. But Dan struck him as some-one who was hanging back and waiting to see which way the wind would blow before committing himself to any one direction. In the meantime, he seemed to be working overly hard to stay on everyone's good side. As a result, Jeff wasn't sure how effective Dan was as a leader in the organization.

Nicole, the CFO, had also been cordial when Jeff arrived, but at the same time, she seemed to intentionally keep her distance, both with him and with the other members of the executive team. Jeff found that disappointing because so far he'd admired her crisp and direct approach to business. She had an ability to explain complicated financial topics in such a clear and concise way that she reminded him of the best of his business school professors. And yet she was a walking contradiction. He had never seen her express much interest in her fellow team members, except when it came to their budgets, but she had a very close relationship with the people who worked under her. It was obvious that she'd earned their utmost trust and respect, and more than once he'd seen an employee pop into her office to ask her advice or just to chat. Jeff sensed that she was very good at running her own department, but he wasn't quite sure why she didn't seem more invested in what was happening among the leadership team.

Manuel, the vice president of sales and marketing, was

the person Jeff knew the least about so far. In Jeff's experience, the kind of people who thrive in sales and marketing positions are talkative and outgoing—extroverted types—but Manuel was just the opposite. He seemed to speak only when spoken to or when he had something critical to say. That wasn't necessarily a problem, but it made Jeff curious. Manuel came across as a very hard worker and when people asked him questions during meetings, he always had the relevant facts and figures ready and an informed opinion to share. But that was where his contributions ended. Jeff wondered if it was because the others tended to blame the company's poor performance on nonspecific "sales and marketing problems." Manuel's department appeared to be taking a lot of heat for things that weren't entirely their fault. Jeff was hoping that after he'd made it clear that he believed the company's problems were everyone's responsibility, and not just one department's, Manuel might open up more. But he really wasn't sure what to expect from him.

Based on these early impressions, Jeff thought Anna and Nicole were likely to be his biggest challenges. With the others, he figured it would just be a matter of helping them understand the value of what he wanted to do so they would become invested in making it happen. He hoped that was the case because if there was one thing he knew for certain it was that he couldn't possibly bring his vision to life all by himself.

Chapter 9

Introducing the team to his new vision for Happy Face Toys was going to be the first step in putting the company on a new course. Despite any reservations he had about how people might react, Jeff couldn't wait to get started. He believed he'd come up with the right idea for getting the company back on track, and it all started with the OGO jar his family had given him. He hadn't expected a birthday present to be his source of inspiration for how to run a company, but sometimes inspiration comes from unexpected places.

With that thought in mind, Jeff entered the conference room where his team had already gathered. He walked up to the front of the room, turned to face the group, and set his OGO jar down on the table in front of him. As he did so, he tried not to read too much into the looks of disinterest on most of their faces.

Jeff took a deep breath and began speaking.

"As you know, I spent Friday in Cleveland, at the very place where Happy Face Toys was founded by my grandfather many years ago. I went there because it has been proposed, by the board and by many of you in this room, that we cut costs by shutting down that facility. Doing so would affect a lot of people, so before I made such an important decision, I needed to see for myself what was happening there and why things haven't been working as well as they used to."

Jeff paused to look at his team. There were still a lot of blank stares, but they appeared to be listening.

"My experience in Cleveland was very enlightening, and it reinforced some of the things I've noticed since I got here about how this company works . . . or doesn't work."

A couple of people seemed to bristle at that, but Jeff continued.

"What I've come to realize is that there are serious problems with how this company functions on many levels. I've seen process problems, a lack of accountability, wasted resources . . ."

"Aren't those all the reasons why the plant should be shut down?" Adam interrupted. He sounded a little impatient, as if he wanted to move the conversation along.

Jeff thought for a moment. He wanted to make himself perfectly clear, to state his observations in such a way that there could be no ambiguity about what he was saying.

"That's just the point I'm trying to make, Adam. The problems I'm describing aren't *just* what's wrong with the plant in Cleveland. I'm talking about what's wrong with how we do things right here in Chicago. And because we're the leaders of this company, our failings are being felt throughout the organization. Cleveland is just a reflection of the bigger picture, of what's happening right here at home."

Adam let out a faint but perceptible snort of disbelief at Jeff's response, and an uncomfortable silence filled the room. Jeff clenched his jaw for a moment, but then decided this was a good thing. He wanted his executive team to feel uncomfortable. Things needed to change, drastically and quickly, and the kind of change he was looking for wasn't going to be comfortable for any of them.

It was Nicole who finally broke the silence. "Can you give us an example of what you mean?" She sounded concerned but not as if she were disagreeing with or challenging him. Jeff was happy to get that much from someone in the group.

Jeff told them about some of the problems he'd witnessed in Cleveland. About the trucks with no drivers and how difficult it had been for people there to navigate the hiring policies set by HR executives in Chicago when they needed someone on the job fast. About the new product ideas that had been sent to the product development department right down the hall that were never responded to. About the family picnics and Employee of the Month ceremonies that had abruptly stopped, he'd learned, when the plant's budget had been slashed by some of the people in this very room. And then he told them about Bob. He told them how a longtime employee of their company, who by all accounts greatly excelled at what he did, had gone his entire forty-seven-year career at Happy Face without ever really feeling appreciated, or even acknowledged, for all his outstanding work.

"It's not our products or our processes or our sales and marketing strategies that are our biggest problem here. Those aren't the main reasons this company is failing." Jeff noticed Manuel sit up a bit straighter in his chair when he said this.

"We have a *Bob* problem. By that I mean we have a serious people problem here at Happy Face Toys if someone like Bob, who has added so much value to the company, doesn't feel as if its leadership cares about or appreciates him in return. That's no way to motivate people or get the best out of them. It's no way to inspire people to contribute more or tackle tough issues. And we're going to need *everyone* giving it their all if we're going to turn this company around."

Jeff paused for a moment to let that sink in. As he glanced around the room, he thought a couple of people were really thinking about what he'd said, but Adam still looked skeptical and Anna appeared downright disapproving. Not unexpectedly, she was the first to react.

"Jeff, I don't mean to be contrary. I know you want this company to succeed as much as we do, but I have to disagree with you. We may not be the best at motivating people or showing them we care, but it's hardly the biggest problem we face. You just got here, so maybe you don't realize how consistently our sales figures have declined year after year. I know people in the tech business where you come from love to talk about things like free lunches and open office concepts and the importance of all that 'culture' stuff, but companies like the one you came from also have money to burn. We're not in that position. We could have the happiest people in the world working here, but it's not going to matter if we go out of business. And that's a real possibility."

Jeff had heard Anna speak this way more than once since he'd arrived at the company, as if she were having to explain something that ought to have been perfectly obvious to a child. But it was the first time she'd directed that tone toward him, and it set his teeth on edge. He had to remind himself that he wasn't looking for a fight; he was looking for allies. So he took a deep breath before responding.

"That's true, of course. None of this matters if we go out of business. And frankly, I hate the word 'culture' too. It sounds too much like a germ. What we're really talking about here is what kind of work environment we're creating for our people," Jeff said, pausing for a moment to gauge Anna's reaction. She appeared stone-faced, so he continued, "But I think we disagree about why the sales figures are falling. So far, the only way we have tried to remedy that problem is by introducing new sales strategies and marketing initiatives. And time and time again, those efforts have failed. Why do you think that is?"

"Because sales and marketing haven't hit on the right strategy yet," Anna responded with absolute certainty.

Manuel, as the head of sales and marketing, shot Anna a withering look, but she didn't seem to notice. Or maybe she just didn't care.

"I think the idea that we have to find the perfect sales strategy to be our magic bullet or else the whole company fails is a pretty risky way to do business," Jeff answered quickly before words could start between Anna and Manuel. "Besides, say we *are* lucky enough to find the perfect sales strategy that lifts us out of our slump. What happens after that? After all, no sales strategy works forever, so we'll be right back where we started in due time. We need to do much more than rely on some mythical sales strategy to make this company a success. And we need to start by fixing what I see as a systematic, company-wide problem with how our people feel about working here."

Anna was shaking her head as if she just didn't get it, so Jeff continued. "Let me give you an example of what I mean. I told you how Cleveland hasn't been able to get drivers for their trucks quickly enough. That is a highly solvable problem. And yet it's been going on for months. Why? They've sent us reports. Calls have been made. This is a known issue, and yet it's still going on. Why hasn't it been solved yet?"

Jeff paused for a moment to see if anyone would attempt an answer. When no one did, he stifled a sigh before offering one himself.

"I believe the real reason this problem remains unsolved is that no one cares enough to see it through, to make sure it gets solved—no one in Cleveland and no one here either."

Jeff let that statement hang in the air for a while too. If he thought his team was uncomfortable before, he really felt it now. Part of him thought it served them right, but the other part knew he'd have to try even harder. The conclusions he'd drawn from his experiences in Cleveland had seemed so obvious to him, but they clearly weren't having the same impact on the group in Chicago. He reminded himself that he was asking them to look at the business in an entirely new way, and it was going to take time for that to happen. The problem was he didn't have a lot of time to get this right. The board had only given him a year to make the kind of major changes he was envisioning.

"Can I ask a question?" Dan asked, half raising his hand.

"Of course," Jeff answered, relieved that someone was chiming in.

"What is that thing?" Dan pointed to Jeff's OGO jar. It was still sitting on the conference table in front of them, but so far it had gone unacknowledged.

"I'm glad you asked," Jeff replied. This seemed like as good a time as any to transition into a more positive view of the company's future. "It's a symbol of how I want us to fix our people problem so that we can move forward together."

"How's that?" Dan asked, dumbfounded.

Jeff went on to explain the experience he'd had over the weekend of receiving the OGO jar from his family. He described as clearly as he could what it meant to him to receive such a simple yet personal gift. He even opened it up and read a few of the messages aloud to give them the idea.

After doing so, Jeff looked up and was pleased to see a few members of the group with genuine smiles on their faces, Manuel and Nicole among them. He wanted to hear what they thought, what was making them smile like that, but before he could ask, Anna piped up again.

"Again Jeff, not to be contrary," Anna began. Jeff was starting to think Anna only knew how to be contrary, but he held his tongue.

"I want to make sure I have this straight," Anna continued. "This jar, full of paper messages or whatever, is what you see as the key to our future success as a company? I have to tell you, I just don't get it," Anna said flatly. She didn't bother to hide her cynicism, and no one was smiling now. In fact, everyone was looking at Jeff to see how he would handle this challenge.

Jeff took yet another deep breath. He didn't want his answer to sound angry even though Anna's insistence on being critical was really getting on his nerves. If she had even once offered a real solution to any of the problems the company was facing, then he might be able to stomach it, but all she seemed to contribute were biting remarks.

"The short answer," Jeff replied, keeping his voice steady and looking her directly in the eye, "is yes. That's exactly what I'm saying." Jeff thought he heard someone in the room muffle a gasp. He ignored it and continued his explanation.

"What you need to understand is that this jar is about a whole lot more than some nice words on pieces of paper. It's an example of something that's obviously been missing around here, and we're going to need more of it if we want to get this company back on track. It's something that's going to make our people *want* to fix the kinds of problems that are happening in Cleveland. Something that's going to make them *eager* to contribute the kind of new thinking and innovative ideas that every company needs to succeed. Something that's going to help us share knowledge and tackle problems *together,* rather than competing against or blaming one another for what's going wrong. When it comes to things like problem solving, innovation, knowledge sharing, or working together as a team, is there anyone in this room who thinks we currently excel in these areas?"

As skeptical as they were of his ideas, Jeff had them there. None of them could claim excellence in any of these areas. Even though no one said anything, he did see a few heads shaking as if to say, "No, we don't."

"We've got to shake things up," Jeff told them. "That means shocking the system. We can't be like every other company in the world. We're the Happy Face Toy Company, and we have to start acting like it. We have to start having some fun, start celebrating our people and everything they can do to turn this company around. If we can do that, then good things will start to happen." Still no one said anything. Jeff would have liked to have heard some words of support, but at least no one was protesting. He decided he wasn't going to hold back. He was going to lay it all out then and there and see what happened.

"When I left Cleveland on Friday, I was pretty depressed

about what I'd seen. I'd encountered problem after problem after problem, and all I could think was, how am I ever going to fix all this? After all, I'm the new guy. I just got here, and I don't even know that much about the toy business. Then it hit me: *I* am not going to fix all those problems. At least not alone. What my job is really all about is inspiring *others* to fix those problems, and making sure they have what they need to get their job done. I don't claim to be the best business leader in the world or an expert in toy manufacturing, but that doesn't matter because even the best leader couldn't do it alone. We all need people to succeed. So the question becomes, how do we get people to help us?"

Jeff had been building to this moment. He paused for a few seconds before introducing the cornerstone of his plan to turn the company around. It was a simple idea, but a profound one, and he wanted to make sure they really heard it.

"The answer is something you've probably all heard about before. But it's something I've found is lacking in all corners of this company, and I really believe we're suffering for it. The answer is *recognition*."

Jeff saw a few raised eyebrows, but he continued his explanation before anyone could interrupt.

"Recognition is the tool we're going to use to get people excited about making this company succeed again. I'm

59

going to use the OGO jar I received as inspiration for a CEO's award to recognize outstanding contributions to the company. I'm going to use it to get the ball rolling, to get people reinvested in the company's success and foster a spirit of teamwork and innovation that will not only turn things around, but also propel us forward. That's where I'm going to start, but for this to really work, I need every one of you to participate as well and to get your departments to participate in making recognition a bedrock of how we do business. Recognition is going to be everyone's top priority from now on."

Jeff paused again to take a breath. It was time to drive his point home.

"The bottom line is this: we have a huge challenge ahead of us. Our sales are down seven percent. Worse yet, they've been down for five straight years in a row, so our profits are in even worse shape. We need to turn the company around so that instead of losing ground year after year, we can start growing again. That's something we all want to see happen. That's something we all *need* to see happen if we want to keep afloat and keep our jobs. In order to do that, we have to make some radical changes. If we can't make someone like Bob, who has given so much to this company, feel as if he has a real place and real value in this organization, then we're dead in the water. Who would ever want to work for a company like that? How are we ever going to motivate our people to go the extra mile in an atmosphere like that? Our company's mission is 'to put a smile on every child's face.' How are we supposed to do that if we can't make even our best people feel good about working here? There's no way. It simply won't happen. That's why I want this to be the last time good work goes unnoticed or unappreciated at the Happy Face Toy Company."

Jeff looked around the room then, taking in each of his team members one by one. He was issuing them a challenge. The question now was whether they would step up to the plate.

Chapter 10

After Jeff finished speaking, he asked his team if they had any question or comments about his new recognition-based vision for the company. No one had any, but he knew he had made his point. The trick now would be in the doing. So he wrapped up the meeting and let everyone go, asking them all to go back and really internalize his message for themselves.

As they were leaving the room, Adam stopped him and asked, "Does this mean you're not going to shut down the Cleveland plant?"

Jeff wasn't surprised that Adam had cut right to chase, but he wished the question had been something about recognition or the unsolved problems in Cleveland.

"Yes, Adam, it means I'm not going to shut down the plant," Jeff responded. "Not now. And hopefully, if things work out the way I'm envisioning, not ever."

"Have you told the board about this?" Adam asked.

"Let me worry about the board," Jeff said.

"I just can't help wondering how they're going to react to the news. Not only are we not doing what they've recommended, but we're going to focus our efforts instead on this warm and fuzzy recognition thing you're proposing. All while Rome is burning. Don't you think they're going to have some questions?"

"The board has given me permission to pursue a new strategy, and this is the strategy I'm committed to. I said it before, but I'll say it again: the way this company has been run for the past several years simply isn't working. The board knows that, and that's why they've given me leeway to take us in a new direction."

Adam just stared at him for a moment. Jeff thought he was about to say something more, but then he shrugged his shoulders, turned, and walked away.

Well that could have gone better, Jeff thought to himself as he walked back to his office. He wasn't just thinking about his run-in with Adam; he was thinking about the entire meeting. The look on Jeff's face must have been telling because when he walked into his office, Marjorie followed him inside and shut the door behind her.

"How did it go?" she asked softly. "Is there anything you need? Anything I can do?"

Marjorie had proved to be a real ally so far even though Jeff hadn't been the one to hire her. She'd worked for his father before him, and at first Jeff thought she would probably retire when his father passed away. Instead, she'd stayed on to help him with his transition. Jeff always suspected it was out of loyalty to his father, but he was happy to have her, whatever the reason. Now he looked at her concerned face and decided it might be a good idea to confide in her. After all, she seemed to have a good sense of the dynamics at play in the organization, and she might have some useful insights.

"Well," Jeff began, "why don't you have a seat. I could use your opinion."

Jeff then explained everything to her: his experiences in Cleveland, what had happened with Bob, his OGO jar, and finally his plan to make recognition a way of life at Happy Face Toys so that people would feel valued and motivated to produce better results in whatever way they could in their own corner of the business. To Jeff's surprise, Marjorie's reaction was not just positive, it was effusive.

"I'm so glad to hear you say these things," she told him. "I think it's exactly what we need."

"You may think so, and I think so, but I'm not so sure the team agrees with us. The reactions I just got in my meeting with them were quite the opposite of yours. It was mostly a mixture of undermining comments and passive silences."

"They may not *want* to make the kind of changes you're

describing, but they *need* to make them. I've been here a long time and I remember when there was a real communal spirit in this office, everyone working together as a team, supporting each other, enjoying what they did and each other in the process. Not only was it a more pleasant place to work back then, but the company was also in a better place. And I don't think that was a coincidence. But now it's all about finger-pointing and backstabbing and jockeying for power . . ."

Marjorie paused then, as if wondering whether she should continue.

"You may not know this . . ." Marjorie began, looking at Jeff for a reaction.

"Go on," Jeff prompted her. He had no idea what she was about to tell him, but he had a feeling it was important.

"Well, you see, your father was sick for quite a while before he passed," Marjorie said. "I know you knew about his illness, but I don't think he ever really told you how bad it was or for how long he'd been fighting it."

"That sounds like dad," Jeff said with a sad smile. Jeff's father had always been a proud man, the type of person who preferred to focus on other people and not on himself. Because they lived so far apart, Jeff hadn't picked up on the fact that his father was downplaying his illness, but the news didn't come as a complete surprise.

"You know your father," Marjorie continued, her voice

filled with sympathy. "He didn't want to worry you too much. And he didn't want anyone around here finding out because he was afraid they would ask him to step down. The problem was, after he got sick, he started spending less and less time here. It wasn't his fault, but things began to slip. He had a strong team, and he thought they would rise to the occasion. Unfortunately, that's not what happened. They may not have known he was sick, but I think they sensed the vacuum created in his absence. Some retreated without him here to lead them, and others began vying for power. When he died, I know of at least two people on the team who wanted your position—badly. They were more than a little upset when the board chose you to fill your father's shoes."

"I didn't know that," Jeff said, stunned by the news. He thought for a moment, and then said, "If that's the kind of politics that's been going on around here, maybe it's hopeless. Maybe the only way to turn things around is to clean house and start anew."

"I don't think it's hopeless," Marjorie said. "Remember, these people were hired by your father for a reason. I think they've just lost their way and need to be shown a new path. You have to keep in mind that things weren't always like this."

Jeff thought about that for a moment and then said,

"Maybe what they need, what we all need, is to be reminded of where we came from."

"What do you mean?" Marjorie asked.

"I mean taking them back to the place where this company started. Maybe the team needs to experience for themselves what I experienced last week when I visited Cleveland."

Marjorie smiled at her boss. "I think that's a great idea." Then she added, "Sometimes you remind me so much of your father when he was younger."

"Thanks, Marjorie. I can see why my father relied so heavily on you. You've been a great sounding board."

"Glad I could help," Marjorie said, getting up to leave. "I'll get started on the arrangements for Cleveland right away."

♛ ♛ ♛

For the rest of the day, Jeff debated the best way to tell the team he was taking them on a trip to Cleveland. At first, he thought about simply sending out an email telling them their presence was required for a full day the following week. But he knew that would be taking the easy way out. He'd always hated how people so often used email in business as a way of avoiding conflict. If he was really going to change their minds about how to run the company, he needed to meet them face to face to let them see how important the trip was to him and to their future with the company, so he scheduled another team meeting for the very next day.

Everyone was already gathered in the conference room when Jeff walked in on Tuesday afternoon. And once again, he was greeted with a host of blank stares. Jeff ignored them and launched right into his pitch.

"I want to announce to you all that we'll be taking a trip together next week to Cleveland. We're going to visit the place where this company started, and I'm going to introduce you to the people I met there last week. This will give you a chance to experience for yourselves what I experienced there."

The silence was deafening. Jeff was starting to wonder if there was something wrong with these people. He was really sick and tired of feeling as if he were all alone in these meetings, but he'd made a decision to stay positive, so he forced a smile onto his face before asking, "Any questions?"

Adam finally said, "I'm just wondering, with everything that's going on here, do you really think we have time for this?"

"I need you to make time," Jeff said. "This is important."

"What day is this happening?" Anna asked. "Because

I have to say I'm with Adam on this. My team is in the middle of a big project, and I'm concerned that—"

"It's happening on Monday. Just one day out of your schedules," Jeff responded before Anna could finish saying what he knew she was about to say, which was some version of "I don't have time for this."

"Any team worth its salt should be able to manage on its own without its leader for a day," he added. He knew he was being blunt, but it was also the truth. And it seemed to him that his team could use a bit more truth telling.

"I have a pretty important meeting on Monday," Dan piped up, as if to jump on the bandwagon.

"Then you'll have to reschedule it. This trip is about getting the company back on track, and there's no higher priority than that. I said it before and I'll say it again: what we've been doing isn't working. It's time—past time—to try a new tack. And that's exactly what we're going to start doing on Monday."

When no one said anything further, Jeff asked, "Any more questions?" A couple of heads shook no.

"Great, then I'll see you all in Cleveland on Monday. Marjorie will be sending you the details." With that, Jeff turned and walked out of the room.

Chapter 11

Back in his office, Jeff was considering giving up for the day. It felt as if he were beating his head against the same wall over and over again, and not surprisingly, it was giving him a headache. He thought the best thing he could do right now was get a little distance from the office and clear his head.

He was just about to text his wife to see if she wanted to meet him for an early dinner at their favorite restaurant when Marjorie called out to him from her desk. "Jeff, Nicole is here to see you."

Jeff was so surprised by Marjorie's announcement that he got up from his desk and walked to the door to make sure he'd heard her right. Sure enough, there was Nicole standing there.

"Oh, hi Nicole," Jeff said, unable to hide his surprise. "What can I do for you?"

"I was wondering if I could talk to you for a minute," Nicole said.

Oh no, Jeff thought, what new objections could she possibly have? He thought he had heard them all already.

But what he said was, "Sure, come on in."

Nicole looked uncomfortable as she sat down in a chair opposite Jeff. She looked at him for a moment before launching into a speech that sounded more than a little rehearsed.

"I just wanted you to know," Nicole began, "that I truly believe in what you're trying to do. I know the team has been difficult about it, and there are those who have their doubts. Strong doubts. But I thought it was important to tell you that I'm not one of them. I think the kind of change you're proposing is something that's been a long time coming around here."

Jeff was stunned. This was not what he was expecting to hear from her at all. She typically didn't say much during meetings, and Jeff had taken her silence to mean she agreed with the general direction of the group.

"I really appreciate you telling me this, but I have to tell you, I'm also surprised. I wouldn't have guessed that you agreed with me based on what has been said in the room. I have to ask, why haven't you spoken up before?"

"Self-preservation," Nicole said with a hint of sarcasm.

"What do you mean?" Jeff prompted.

"The kinds of things you've been talking about—about using one's position as a leader to make sure people know they matter, to inspire them to aim higher and reach their full potential, to recognize their accomplishments, not only for their own sake, but also to drive results in a positive way—those are the kinds of values I've been working to instill in my own team since the day I got here."

"I've noticed that you're tight with your team members. They clearly think very highly of you."

"I've worked hard to earn that from them. And I continue to work at it every day. I've always believed that making sure my people have what they need—in terms of real resources, of course, but also in a kind of spiritual way, by feeling motivated and appreciated and inspired— that's the most important part of my job. But in the past, when I've talked about such things with the executive team—"

"What's happened?"

"Frankly, they've shut me down. When I've tried to remind them of the company's mission, for example, they say things like, 'What we need is more sales, not more smiles.' I've always believed those two things go together, but the team doesn't share my opinion. So I've learned to keep my mouth shut around them and then just do what I needed to do when it came to leading my own team."

Jeff was struck by the passion with which Nicole talked about her people. He suddenly realized that they were a lot alike and were facing many of the same barriers. "It must be hard for you to work like that," Jeff said with newfound sympathy.

"It is. We've got some pretty strong naysayers in our midst."

"You mean about the changes I'm trying to make?" Jeff asked.

"I mean about everything," Nicole clarified. "I've always thought it was their way of protecting themselves, of saying, 'The company may be failing, but it's not *my* fault.' When really we're all at fault if the company fails. But since I've always been the odd woman out, I've kept those thoughts to myself."

"Well, I'm glad you didn't keep those thoughts from me. I appreciate your candor, Nicole. I really do. I think I understand things a bit better now. And it's especially good to know that I'm not alone in this."

Nicole smiled at him to let him know that was true.

"But I also want to ask you for your help. I hope I can count on you to be more forthcoming in the future, not just with me but with everyone. If things are going to change around here, it's going to take all of us, and I could use some help convincing the others."

Nicole sighed at that. "I'm not going to lie to you. I've

gotten to know these people pretty well, and it's going to be an uphill battle."

Jeff was worried she was going to backtrack, but then she said, "But it's a battle worth fighting."

"So can I count on your support?"

"Yes, you can," Nicole said with conviction. "Part of me is dreading the confrontation that's coming, but another part of me can't wait to see how it turns out. If there was ever a group that needed shaking up, it's this one."

"That's exactly what I'm hoping will happen in Cleveland," Jeff said.

Chapter 12

When Jeff arrived back in Cleveland only a week and a half after his first visit, he felt a keen sense of anticipation about what he was about to do. He'd asked all the plant employees to gather in the warehouse just as before. When he walked in with his team, there were the same folding chairs scattered about and an even larger makeshift stage up front, this time consisting of several shipping crate tops. As he made his way through the crowd, he received more than a few hellos and welcoming smiles, a stark contrast to how he'd been greeted the last time around.

Jeff left his team standing at the side as he walked to the center of the stage to kick off the meeting. He carried with him a large paper bag, which he set down on the floor next to him.

"Thank you all for joining me once again," he began. "As I mentioned last time I was here, our company is facing some big challenges. If we want to thrive in today's marketplace, we're going to have to make some big changes. I came back with my whole team today because I want those changes to start right here and right now."

Jeff looked out over the group and was pleased to see that he had their rapt attention. This was a very different crowd from the one he'd introduced himself to more than a week before. In such a short amount of time, there hadn't been much progress made on any of the issues they'd discussed, but they still seemed pleased he was there. It was amazing to Jeff that all he'd had to do was make them feel heard and take their concerns seriously to start earning their trust and respect. Of course to keep their trust and respect he knew he'd have to deliver on his promises, but for now they were giving him the benefit of the doubt. He didn't take that for granted, and he really didn't want to let any of them down.

"Based on our last conversation and what I saw during my visit here, I believe many of you feel as if you've been forgotten about or left behind by the company as a whole. That's our fault," he said gesturing to his team, "and I don't want it to happen anymore. One of the ways I'm going to ensure that it doesn't is by changing our priorities. Not enough attention has been paid to the simple but critical idea that all of us are in this together and striving to realize the same mission of 'putting a smile on every child's face.' I believe that's a noble goal, and none of us can do it alone.

"To help us regain focus on that mission, I'm going to make some changes in the way we do things at Happy Face Toys. And I'm going to start with something that was inspired by my grandson." Jeff then told them about his OGO jar and what it had meant to him to feel so valued and appreciated by his family.

"It was a gift I never would have asked for, but it was still one of the greatest gifts I've ever received. I got so much out of those simple expressions of appreciation that I wanted to do the same for others. After my last visit here, I realized we need a lot more of that around here. We need more appreciation, more inspiration, more motivation, and especially more recognition of our people if we want to have a hope of becoming a world-class company again. I want that spirit to become the cornerstone of our work environment moving forward, and I'm going to start by instituting the CEO's award so I can recognize people who are making outstanding contributions to this company whenever and wherever I see it."

Jeff paused then to search for a specific face in the crowd. When he found it, he continued. "Bob, I want *you* to be the recipient of the very first CEO's award."

A murmur ran through the crowd as Jeff turned to the

paper bag still sitting on the floor next to him. He reached inside and pulled out something that instantly made people in the front row smile. It was a simple glass jar with the word "OGO" printed in big bold letters across the front of it, and "O Great One" in smaller letters underneath. It was his own version of his grandson's OGO jar, and inside he'd put messages that he had quietly solicited from some of Bob's closest colleagues describing what they thought was so great about him and why they appreciated him. Jeff had also included a handwritten letter thanking Bob personally for all he'd done for the company. At the bottom, he'd signed and dated the letter, followed by a note welcoming Bob to the "club of OGOs." He planned to do the same for every OGO Award he gave out, and he intended to give one to every single person he met who was making an outstanding contribution to the company.

Jeff held out the jar to Bob and said, "This is the OGO Award, inspired by my own family, and given to you because you've proved to the family of people in this room that you're an OGO to all of us. I know this thank-you is long overdue. In fact, because you're retiring this week, it almost comes too late, but it is no less sincere. Before you leave us here at Happy Face, I want you to know how much everyone appreciates you. I want you to know that we think of you as one of the Great Ones!"

With that the crowd erupted into applause. Everyone

stood up, and Bob was both beaming and laughing as he walked up to the stage to accept his award. Then, with a twinkle in his eye and a huge smile on his face, he turned to face the crowd and held his OGO jar in the air high above his head as if he'd just won the Super Bowl.

In that moment the noise from the crowd grew even louder. Jeff could tell that the people in the room were really starting to believe things could be different. That filled him with a much-needed sense of hope. As he looked out over the crowd, he couldn't help but think: just wait, *you* haven't seen anything yet.

Chapter 13

Jeff had anticipated that this moment would mean a lot to Bob, but even he hadn't foreseen just how much the rest of the crowd would get into it. Everyone was cheering as Jeff took a picture with Bob holding his OGO Award. Jeff then explained to Bob, as well as the rest of the crowd, that since taking over as CEO, he hadn't yet had time to decorate his new office. He was finally going to start by making the walls of his office into his own personal OGO gallery. Every time he gave out an award, he planned to take a picture with the recipient, have that picture framed, and then hang it on his walls.

"I can't think of anything I'd rather look at every day than the people who are helping to make this company great," he told them. "You are what's going to inspire me above all else." When Jeff looked over at Bob, he saw that once again Bob had tears in his eyes. But this time Jeff knew they were tears of joy.

Jeff thanked Bob one more time before Bob returned to his seat so Jeff could continue with the meeting. "That's not all I want to accomplish here today," Jeff said in an attempt to refocus the room. He was thrilled with the reaction to his recognition award, but that was just the first step. "I wanted to give out the first OGO Award here today, not just because Bob is such a deserving recipient—which he certainly is," Jeff turned and smiled at Bob once more. "But I also did it in the hope of inspiring you all because now, once again, I need to ask for your help. To make the kind of change I'm looking for in the way this company works, I can't be the only person promoting a spirit of recognition. I'm just one man, after all, and this is a big company. So I'm also challenging everyone in the company, at every level, to make recognition part of their daily activities in whatever way works best for them and for the people they work with. Is that something we think we can make happen around here?"

Jeff looked out at the crowd and his faith in them was met with more cheers and applause.

"Good. I'm glad to hear it. I also want to thank all of you for your helpful insights into what wasn't working for the company the last time I was here. I got a lot out of that discussion, so much in fact that I brought my entire team back with me to address the problems we discussed and any others you can think of. This is *our* company, all of ours, and we want to hear what you have to say about how we can make it better."

Jeff hadn't prepared his team for this on purpose. He wanted to see how they would react under fire. He motioned for them to join him, and one by one they lined up across the front of the makeshift stage. By the look on some of their faces, you might have thought he was asking them to stand in front of a firing squad. Jeff couldn't help but grin just a little at that. He'd been in this same position himself when he'd faced these people for the first time a little more than a week before, and he remembered how it felt.

"Who wants to go first?" Jeff asked the crowd. He had to stifle another grin when Gabriel was first to raise his hand.

Gabriel brought up the now familiar issue of the missing truck drivers, a question that, because he was head of operations, was put to Dan. Dan stumbled through a response, trying to bring in Adam, who had approved their hiring policies, but who quickly deflected the question back to Dan. It was obvious Dan didn't have anything helpful to say on the matter, so Jeff stepped in and said, "Clearly, Gabriel, we are going to have to make some changes to our hiring policies. Now that Dan fully understands the issue, he can start working on that as soon as he gets back to Chicago. Right Dan?" Dan nodded, looking relieved.

"So, what else?" Jeff asked.

Next, Carmen raised the issue of the budget cuts that had led to the loss of some of their favorite perks, such as the annual picnic and monthly Employee of the Month celebrations.

Jeff was pleased to see Nicole step forward. "Hi Carmen, I'm Nicole, and as the company's CFO, I bear primary responsibility for many of the budget cuts that have been imposed. I want you to know that I hear what you're saying. It's hard to feel invested in the company you work for when it feels like that company isn't invested in you. I get that. And it's possible that our cuts may have been too extreme. In an effort to free up some resources, we may have ended up tying your hands, and that wasn't our intention. I'm going to have some members of my team review our budget cuts and see if we can't find enough funds for you to spruce things up around here and get back some of those important team-building activities that have meant so much to you. After all, our new CEO has said that appreciating our people and recognizing their good work is a top priority at Happy Face, and we all need to play our part in supporting that idea, here and back in Chicago."

Jeff thought that was a pretty good answer, but Nicole wasn't done. She paused for a moment to let her promise sink in, and then she continued. "At the same time, I want to challenge all of you to think creatively. As we witnessed here today with Bob, it doesn't have to cost a lot to make someone feel appreciated. I believe that even small gestures can have a big impact on people."

"Hear, hear!" Bob called from the audience.

Nicole smiled at him and then continued. "In my experience, two of the most powerful words in the English language are 'thank' and 'you,' and saying those words to someone doesn't cost a thing. This company is facing some tough financial times, and we're all going to have to tighten our belts a little to get through it. But that's no reason to stop appreciating each other or rewarding good work in whatever way we can."

Jeff was impressed. A number of people in the crowd even applauded Nicole's answer, and Carmen thanked her for it. It was exactly the kind of exchange Jeff had being hoping for but hadn't been so sure he would get. He was wondering now if perhaps he should have had a little more faith in his own people.

The Q&A continued with an intense back-and-forth that lasted nearly two hours, during which Jeff remained mostly silent. By watching the exchange, he learned a lot about the people on his team. Adam largely stayed above the fray, answering only those questions posed directly to him. Even then, he would deftly deflect to someone else or cut the conversation short with a noncommittal phrase such as "That's an issue I would have to look into more fully in order to answer your question." Dan fumbled a few more questions about purchasing issues and process problems, making Jeff wonder whether he really had a handle on his responsibilities as the head of operations. Anna, not surprisingly, spent most of the time looking bored—except when someone from engineering asked a question about why there wasn't better coordination between the IT systems in Cleveland and Chicago. Anna immediately got defensive and said that she already knew about the problem and had her best people working on it.

Fortunately, Nicole fielded a few more questions with the same ease as the first one. But the real standout, much to Jeff's surprise, was Manuel. The normally introverted VP of sales and marketing came alive on stage, willingly taking part in the conversation, even on issues that didn't directly affect his department. He was quick to thank people and praise a good idea when he heard one. He asked questions in return, appearing to take a genuine interest in what people did and thought and how things worked there, in Cleveland. He even asked Bob if he'd be willing to come to Chicago to meet with him one-on-one and talk about all the great merchandising ideas he'd been hearing so much about.

After Jeff called an end to the meeting and thanked everyone for their participation, it was Manuel who was surrounded by people wanting to talk more. Anna and Adam stood awkwardly to the side as person after person walked right past them to get to Manuel. When Jeff suggested it was time for them all to head to the airport, Manuel actually looked disappointed. Jeff wasn't entirely sure what to make of his transformation.

He couldn't help but wonder, *Where has this Manuel been all this time?* He was definitely going to have to ask Manuel that question as soon as he got the chance.

Chapter 14

On the flight back to Chicago, reactions from his team members were mixed. Nicole and Manuel chatted together amiably, with Dan joining in on occasion. Anna stared out the window and said barely anything to anyone at all. Adam pulled out his laptop and started pounding furiously on his keyboard. No one dared interrupt him during the duration of the flight even though his pounding made quite a racket.

Despite the mixed reactions, Jeff considered the day a success. He knew it would take time for his team to adapt to his ideas, but he felt the experience in Cleveland must have made an impression on even the most resistant among them.

Back in his office the next day, Jeff was still going through what had happened in his head. Much of it had turned out the way he'd expected, but there had been one big thing he hadn't anticipated—Manuel. Why did this guy who had always been so quiet seem like a new man when interacting with the people in Cleveland? Jeff didn't know the answer, but he was interested in finding out.

He put in a call to Manuel. His VP didn't answer, but on his voice mail Jeff left a message asking him to come by for a chat when he had a free moment during the day. It was barely ten minutes later when Manuel appeared at his door. "Is now a good time?" he asked.

Jeff said yes and motioned for Manuel to sit down. Because Jeff was the one who'd asked for the meeting, he expected to speak first, but before Manuel had finished taking his seat, he launched right in.

"Sir, before anything else, I just wanted to thank you. I really appreciate the opportunity we had yesterday. I think it was good for me. For all of us really, but especially for me."

"Why do you say that?" Jeff asked.

"Last week, when you started talking about making changes around here and using recognition to do it, well, it's not like I didn't think you had good ideas. It's just . . ."

"Go on," Jeff prompted. "I really want to hear what you have to say."

"Well, I guess I just didn't think recognition could possibly be a top priority. I've always believed that it's the hard things, the things you can measure, that really drive results. Like how many times we have to contact a prospect before we can convert him to a sale. Or what pricing strategy leads to the highest sales volume. So I felt like I couldn't afford to recognize people until after we'd turned the business around. I was worried people would take their foot off the gas if I focused on their achievements rather than on how much work we needed to do to move the needle. So that's what I've been focusing on, especially since our sales have started to decline . . ."

Manuel turned away from Jeff then with a guilty look on his face. Jeff was getting the feeling that Manuel really did believe the company's troubles were all his fault. He also suspected that the rest of the team had let him believe that.

"Those things *are* important to focus on, Manuel. But you can't wait until you score a touchdown to celebrate. You've got to celebrate the first downs along the way because that's what keeps people going. It's both the hard *and* the soft things that get results. For example, what motivates your salespeople to go the extra mile to reach a potential new customer? And what keeps that customer coming back? It's not just about having the best prices or products. It's also about the intangibles, such as customer service, relationships, being the kind of company that others enjoy dealing with. And that all starts with our people. If they don't enjoy working here, if they don't feel appreciated, then how can we expect them to pass those things on to the customers?"

"I agree with you," Manuel said readily. "I mean, I agree with you now. I think I've just been distracted. I guess I needed to see your ideas in action to understand just how important they were. When I saw the look on Bob's face when you gave him that award, and the way the crowd responded, I really got it. I mean, all those people who weren't even being recognized were so obviously moved to see someone else being rewarded, especially someone so deserving. They couldn't stop talking about it afterward. The whole thing just . . ."

"Just what?"

"It fired me up!" It was obvious to Jeff that Manuel wasn't just trying to get in good with the new boss. Jeff could see that there really was new life in him.

"I'm really glad to hear it. And I also want to thank you."

"Thank me? What for?" Manuel looked confused.

"You were great on stage yesterday. You really helped make the day meaningful for all those people who took time out of their day to be there and tell us what they thought. I was so impressed by how you interacted with everyone. I could tell they really felt that you heard them and respected what they had to say."

"It means a lot to hear you say that. I have to admit, I never would have taken the time to do what we did yesterday on my own. But I'm really glad I had the opportunity to hear what they had to say. They came up with some great ideas."

"They did, and we always need to remember that. The best ideas aren't always going to come out of this office."

Manuel nodded at that, and Jeff continued, "I also wanted to ask you why you haven't considered recognizing good work a priority before now?"

Manuel thought about that for a moment, and then said, "It's not that I didn't think it was important. I did, but in business, especially in a struggling business, a lot of things are important. I guess I didn't realize *how* important it was until now. I think it might be because my team tends to get blamed for the problems around here, so trying to avoid that is generally my main focus. Practically my only focus." Manuel paused then to see how Jeff would react to that. When Jeff gave him an encouraging smile, he continued.

"It happens all the time that some new sales or marketing strategy gets put in place because the numbers are down and everyone is demanding change. As a result, my team and I are always scrambling; we're always playing catch-up, trying to find some 'magic bullet,' as you called it the other day, that will put the numbers right. I just didn't think there was time to make something like recognition a priority. But now I see how it can help us cut through a lot of the noise and put the focus where it matters most: on our people. And that's how we'll do better with our customers."

"I agree," Jeff said. "In fact, I think you may have stumbled on a great way to explain what our formula for success should be. First we've got to fire up our people, who will then help to get our customers excited about doing business with us, and from there the money will follow. Too many business leaders focus on making money first without considering the fact that it's people who will make it happen."

"I like that," Manuel agreed. "It makes a lot of sense."

"It does to me too, Manuel. But I think there's another way you can help us all keep the focus where it needs to be."

"What's that?" Manuel asked.

"You can tell the team what you just told me. You can point out that sales and marketing are critical and that you're committed to making your department better than ever, but that it's just one piece of the puzzle. Sure, it's easy to blame sales and marketing when the numbers are down, but that doesn't mean it's always your fault. And believe me, that's the message I will reinforce."

The look of relief on Manuel's face almost made Jeff feel sorry for him. "I have to admit, I feel like the scapegoat in many of our meetings, so I've learned to keep a stiff upper lip and then go back to my team and drive them hard."

"I know you have. You're clearly very smart and you work very hard, but my question is, how has that strategy been working for you so far?"

Manuel thought for a minute, and then admitted, "Not well. Not well at all, actually."

"And how has it been working for the team and the company as a whole?"

"It hasn't," Manuel said, this time without hesitation.

"I'm not going to lie to you, Manuel. You and I know your department is going to have to play a big role in getting this company back on track. But as I told Anna the other day, our problems are bigger than anything some new sales strategy can fix. We have to remake this company from the ground up, and what I've been trying to communicate to all of you is that it's *everyone's* job to do this. It's not just one department that's going to make the difference. It's not just the leadership in each department either. It's every person inside every department stepping up their game and working together. That's what's going to get us there. And that means we need to start by reaching out to all those people and inspiring them to want to take us there."

"I think I understand now."

"I could really use your help driving that point home with the others."

"You've got it, sir."

"And Manuel?"

"Yes?"

"Please call me Jeff. When someone calls me sir, it makes me feel older than I am."

"Of course," Manuel laughed. "You've got it, Jeff."

"Thanks, Manuel. I really appreciate all you've said here today. It means a lot to me, and I think you'll see, as time goes on, that it's going to mean a lot to the whole organization as well."

Chapter 15

Jeff was heartened by his talk with Manuel. His vision was to make recognition the cornerstone of how they did business throughout Happy Face Toys, but he knew that in order to do that, he had to start at the top. If the company's leaders weren't exhibiting the values and behaviors he considered crucial to their success, then how could he expect anyone else to? That's why he had to convince his own team first. And by his count, he now had two out of the five fully on board—Manuel and Nicole.

That left three to go. Jeff didn't feel like taking a wait-and-see approach anymore, so, emboldened by his conversation with Manuel, he decided to force a confrontation with another member of the team whose buy-in was going to be a lot harder to win.

"Marjorie," he said poking his head out of his office, "do you know what Anna is doing today?"

"Let me pull up her calendar." Peering at her computer,

Marjorie said, "It looks like she has a departmental meeting that's just about to start and then she has . . ."

"Perfect, thanks!" Jeff interrupted her.

"What are you going to do?" Marjorie asked with a conspiratorial smile. She could tell her boss was up to something.

"I'm going to crash Anna's meeting."

"Oh, I wish I could see that." Marjorie laughed. "I bet it will get the sparks flying!"

"Don't worry," Jeff reassured her. "I'll tell you all about it when I get back."

When Jeff walked into the IT department, the meeting had already started. A large group of people were gathered in the lounge area, standing about or sitting on couches, and listening to Anna speak.

"We're nearing the end of a tough project, one that we've all been working on for months. We're through the worst part, but I don't want any of you to let up now. Let's bring this thing home. Are there any questions about what's left to do and what the priorities are?"

Jeff hovered on the perimeter of the group as a couple of people asked Anna some technical questions that were over Jeff's head. Several people had noticed Jeff's presence, but Anna hadn't. Jeff leaned toward the person nearest him and whispered, "What's the project you're all finishing up?"

The guy looked at him and smiled. "We've been working on linking the computer systems of all our offices around the globe."

"Sounds like a big job," Jeff responded.

The guy's face lit up when Jeff said this. "Yeah, it has been. And a tricky one too. Because the company's grown so gradually and acquired pieces along the way, there was a whole mess of different systems in place in different locations. It's been crazy trying to get them to speak to one another. But we're nearly there. Soon we'll all be using one integrated system, whether we're in China or Chicago."

"That's pretty great. You must be really proud of yourselves."

The guy snorted a laugh and then glanced over at Jeff. Realizing Jeff was serious, he said, "I guess we are. It's the biggest project I've ever worked on for sure."

"Then that's something to be really proud of," Jeff said.

"Yeah, I guess it is." The guy paused for a moment as if considering the comment. Then he grinned at Jeff and said, "Hey, can I ask you a question? Did you really give some guy in Cleveland a big mason jar as a present?"

"Not exactly." Jeff laughed out loud. He was surprised to hear that news of the OGO Award had spread so quickly. He was also wondering whether it had been described to this guy as a positive or a negative thing. Before he could ask him, Anna was speaking again to the group. Probably because of the noise they'd been making, she had now noticed Jeff's presence, and she didn't look happy.

"So are there any other questions? Anything there in the back?" she said, directing her question toward Jeff.

When no one answered, she said, "All right then, I think we're good. Same time next week. And hopefully by then, if someone here doesn't screw up something, we'll have a completed project to report on."

Jeff stuck around as the crowd dispersed, sensing Anna wanted to speak to him. He was right. As soon as they were out of earshot of the others, Anna said to him bluntly, "I didn't know you were coming."

"It was a last-minute decision. I wanted to check in to see how things were going here. I haven't had much contact with your department since I arrived, and I'd love to get a better sense of what you're all working on."

"I'll be happy to email you an update," Anna responded.

Not willing to be put off so easily, Jeff continued, "I was also wondering what ideas you had come up with for making recognition an important part of how you do things around here."

Anna raised her eyebrows. "I really haven't had a chance to give it much thought. We're finishing this big project, you see, and I already lost Monday . . ."

"Really?" Jeff said. "Some of your people have already heard about the OGO Award, so I thought you had probably discussed it with them."

Anna looked caught off guard by that. She didn't respond but appeared to be more than a little worried about what her people might have said. Jeff decided not to press it.

"I was talking to some of them about this project you're finishing up. Sounds to me like something worth celebrating. A perfect occasion to recognize someone who has gone above and beyond to get it done."

Anna sighed. "Jeff, can I be frank with you?"

"You usually are, Anna," Jeff replied.

"I just don't think that kind of thing is going to work with my staff. These are results-oriented, metric-driven, high-performing team members. That's why I hired them in the first place. They're not the type to go in for all that fluffy stuff. And because we work as a team, singling someone out is just going to make the others jealous. I don't want to motivate one person while demotivating everyone else."

"What I don't think you realize, Anna, is that this isn't fluffy stuff. It's very much about results, about recognizing and rewarding the kind of real results that make a difference to this company's bottom line. And it's about driving future results by sending a clear message about what behaviors lead to results. When we start recognizing the right behaviors, it will fuel the right kind of competition and collaboration among our people."

Anna seemed flustered by that. "I just don't think my people are going to get excited by some old mason jar stuffed with construction paper," she said finally.

Jeff swallowed. He didn't want Anna to see his annoyance, but it seemed to him that she wasn't even trying.

"Anna," Jeff said in a measured tone, "the OGO jar is my award. Yours can be different. In fact, I think it's important for you to come up with something yourself that will have real meaning to the individuals on your team. You seem pretty tight with them. Don't you think you know what matters to them?"

"I guess. I mean, yes, of course I do."

"Great, then I'm sure you'll come up with just the right thing. I'll be back for the celebration next week, and I can't wait to see what it is!"

Chapter 16

A week later, Jeff walked into Anna's office a few minutes before her department meeting. Jeff had purposely not spoken to her after he crashed her IT meeting. He wanted to see how she would meet the challenge he had left her with, if at all.

Marjorie had told Anna he'd be coming by, but she still looked at him as if he were intruding as soon as he entered her office.

Still, his greeting was upbeat. "Hi Anna. I came by to check on plans for your celebration today. Do you know who your OGO is going to be?"

"My OGO?" Anna asked.

"Yes, OGO. It stands for O Great One, remember? That's what I've been calling the people I've been recognizing and celebrating. Like Bob."

"Right, I remember," Anna said.

"Of course you can call your award whatever you want."

"Actually, I do know who I want to call attention to today, and I have come up with something to give him to say thanks. I know he's going to love it."

"Fantastic!" Jeff was a little surprised. He hadn't been so sure that Anna would follow through. In fact, he'd arrived prepared to field excuses. "How did you decide who to give the award to?"

"So many people worked so hard on this project that I felt bad about singling out any one person, so I asked the team to vote on it. Sort of like an MVP Award. They seemed to dig the idea, and there was a hands-down winner." Jeff had never thought about doing it this way, but he didn't have any objections offhand to a peer vote.

"Do you agree with their choice?" he asked her.

"Definitely. He's the shining star of our department."

"Well, great. I can't wait to see how it plays out!"

The team was already assembled in the lounge when Anna and Jeff walked in. Jeff waited on the sidelines while Anna made a few announcements. Then she announced the award presentation.

"As you all know, this was a long, hard project. So at our new CEO's suggestion," Anna gestured halfheartedly toward Jeff, "I'm handing out my first-ever Top Scorer Award. I asked you all to vote on this because so many of you did so much to make this happen, and this person got the vast majority of your votes. Jack, can you come up here, please, to get your award."

As Anna said that, she pulled something out of a box and held it up. It was a miniature old-school video game console with a plaque mounted on the back that read: TOP SCORER: JACK.

There were oohs and aahs mixed with good-natured laughter throughout the room. Jack was beaming as he made his way toward Anna, receiving several pats on the back along the way. When he received his award, Jeff heard him tell Anna, "It's just like a small version of the ones I used to play as a kid! I love it!"

Anna was smiling now, pleased that her award had generated so much enthusiasm. After the presentation, Anna invited everyone to stick around for a little celebration. She had brought in snacks and beer for the occasion.

"Everyone seems to be having a really good time," Jeff said to Anna when he caught her alone.

"Yes," Anna agreed, surveying the room, "and they deserve it. They really did work hard and they did an excellent job."

"And your award was certainly a hit."

"Well, I know my guys," Anna said, smiling to herself. "I knew Jack would love it. He talks all the time about all the video games he used to play at his local pizza parlor as a kid. He likes to joke that it was that experience that made him the man he is today."

"Did you know Jack would win when you decided on the award?"

"Well, I didn't know for sure, but it was a pretty safe bet. He's one of those people who are so great to have on your team because they make everyone better. If someone is stuck, he always has an idea to contribute. Even when he doesn't have the solution, he gets everyone talking and then people don't feel so stuck anymore. And when someone needs help, he's always the first to volunteer. He does everything with such enthusiasm, it's contagious. Everyone loves working with him. So I pretty much knew it would be him."

"That's great," Jeff said. "Sounds like he's a real asset to your team."

"He is," Anna agreed.

"Does he know you think so highly of him?"

Anna paused for a moment. "Well. . . . he must."

"Have you ever told him?"

"Not in so many words."

"Why not?"

Anna stopped then and appeared to be really thinking about the question. Jeff decided he should seize the moment.

"I bet it would be a real shame to lose someone like Jack," he said.

"It would be a huge loss for us," Anna said.

"Have you ever thought about what you can do to encourage him to stick around?"

"It's not like I can give him a raise," Anna shot back, resuming her old defensive stance, "not with budgets as tight as they are."

"No, you can't give him a raise right now, unfortunately, but that's not you're only option. You said that you and your people are metric driven, so you'll appreciate this: studies show that the most common reason people leave their jobs doesn't have anything to do with money at all. It's more often about the environment they work in, about having a tense relationship with their boss or feeling undervalued for the work they do. That's what drives people out the door most of the time."

"Is that true?" Anna asked, looking at Jeff with surprise.

"It is. I'll send you some of the research when I get back to my office." Then he looked at her and added, "That's why it's so important to do things like this, Anna. You may not be able to give Jack a raise right now, but don't you think he feels pretty good today about working here?"

Anna looked over at Jack. He was gesturing in a highly animated way as he told a story to the colleagues surrounding him. Everyone was smiling and laughing at him appreciatively.

"I know he does," Anna conceded.

"I do too," Jeff agreed. "And it's not just about him. It's about everyone here today. Just look around. Everyone's happy and having fun. No one seems upset by not winning an award, but I'm sure many of them are thinking they'd like to be recognized someday too. In the meantime, they're getting a chance to share good feelings with each other and celebrate something they accomplished, something that really matters to this company. *You* created this moment for them, this chance to really feel good about themselves and their work. At the same time, you've shown them what can happen if they really excel. I think, deep down, everyone wants that kind of recognition. It can be really meaningful for people, not to mention motivating. That's why what we really need around here are coaches, not bosses. People don't want to work for bosses; they want to work for people who will help them achieve their potential."

Anna just stood there for a while watching her team. She really did seem to care about her team members, which was something Jeff hadn't noticed about her before. Finally, without looking Jeff in the eye, she said something under her breath so quietly that Jeff almost didn't hear her.

"I guess you're right," she breathed. And then a bit louder. "They really do deserve this."

If Anna had been looking at Jeff then, she surely

would have noticed the look of sheer triumph on his face. Fortunately, she didn't notice, and Jeff decided that this would be a good time to make his exit. He thought it best to quit while he was ahead and leave her and her team to their well-deserved celebration.

As Jeff walked back to his office, he was pleased with how things were shaping up, but he was also intent on taking things even further. He knew he was only beginning to scratch the surface. Anna was just one team member and much more needed to be done to rally the entire team behind him and turn the business around.

Chapter 17

The following day Jeff arrived at the office feeling great. He believed he was finally beginning to gain some momentum. It was clear he still had a long way to go, but for the first time since he'd arrived at Happy Face, it looked as if he might actually be able to make the kinds of changes he wanted.

His optimism got a further boost when Manuel asked him if he would take part in his "surprise recognition party" later that morning. Manuel had identified someone in the sales department who'd had an outstanding quarter, nearly doubling her quota, and he'd come up with the idea of throwing her a surprise party to celebrate her accomplishment. Everyone in the department was going to show up at her desk at a specified time carrying balloons, blowing on plastic horns, and throwing confetti. Then they would all yell "Surprise!" as Manuel presented her with a cake. On it was a picture of the honoree done up in frosting with "Salesperson of the Quarter!" written across the bottom. Manuel thought this would be more fun than just handing her an award and a good way to get everyone involved in the process.

Jeff thought it was a great idea, and when Manuel suggested it would be even more meaningful to everyone if the CEO attended the celebration, he happily agreed. It was a fantastic party, and the recipient of all the attention, Miranda, was not only pleased, she was more than a little sentimental about it. She talked about how much she'd loved her surprise birthday parties when she was a girl and how her mother, who'd passed away the year before, had always made such a big deal about them for her and her sisters. She hadn't told anyone before then about the loss of her mother, and Manuel said it made him realize that he needed to work harder to foster a more open and communal atmosphere in the office. He didn't want his people to think they couldn't talk to him or to their colleagues about things that were clearly so important to them.

It was an incredible event all around, except for one thing. When her colleagues were trying to persuade Miranda to give a little acceptance speech, they pounded on their desks and blew on their plastic horns to encourage her. But before she got a chance, Adam, whose office was just down the hall, came barging in.

"Can you all *please* keep it down out here," he bellowed. "I can hardly hear myself think!"

Adam's face was so red, he looked as if he might blow a blood vessel. His eyes were darting about as if he were looking for someone he could unleash his anger on directly, but then he spied Jeff and abruptly cut his flare-up short. He didn't apologize, however. Instead, he turned on his heel and stormed out of the room. He went back to his office and loudly closed the door.

Jeff was furious. Part of him wanted to follow Adam into his office and give him a piece of his mind right then and there, but he decided it would be better to confront the issue in private after the party had broken up. He didn't want to make a scene or add more negativity to Miranda's celebration, but he knew he couldn't let it go. He couldn't have one of the company's top leaders, his chief legal officer, undermining the very changes he'd been struggling so hard to make, especially in such a public way.

Later that afternoon, after he'd had a chance to calm down and gather his thoughts, Jeff headed to Adam's office to confront him about what had happened and make it clear that Adam's behavior was unacceptable. He also planned to have what was probably an overdue conversation about Adam's communication style in general, about how when he spoke he tended to shut down conversation rather than invite a free and open exchange of ideas. It was something Jeff knew he could work on with Adam if he was only willing to try.

When Jeff arrived at Adam's office, his assistant was out, so Jeff knocked on the door. "What is it?" Adam yelled from inside.

Jeff opened the door and stepped inside. Adam looked surprised to see him, but it was Jeff who spoke first and he got right to the point.

"Hi, Adam. I wanted to talk to you about what happened earlier this morning."

"What are you referring to?" Adam replied evenly.

Jeff wasn't sure whether his CLO was really that oblivious or if he was just playing "lawyer" and challenging Jeff on his claims. Jeff figured it didn't matter either way.

"I'm talking about what happened during Manuel's party to celebrate his Salesperson of the Quarter."

"Is that what that was? I just heard all the noise. I didn't know what it was about."

"It was about recognizing someone who has done outstanding work for this company, and it really dampened the celebration when you came in yelling like that. I want our people to feel as if they're appreciated for what they do, and I have to tell you, I think your behavior conveyed the exact opposite message."

"But they're not even my people," Adam protested.

"It doesn't matter," Jeff replied. "You're one of the

leaders of this company, and the way you act sends a message to others about what we value and what kind of behavior we allow. My grandfather used to call this 'the shadow of the leader.' If people see the leadership acting in a certain way or not taking part in something, then they think it's OK for them to do the same, even when they've been told explicitly to do the opposite. It comes down to actions speaking louder than words. You're a leader in this organization and, like it or not, you cast a big shadow. On everyone, not just those who report to you. You have to be conscious of that fact in everything you do. People are watching you, so I need you to make sure with your words *and* your actions, that you are casting the right shadow."

"But they were making it hard for me to do *my* job. I didn't have a choice."

"You did have a choice, Adam. You had a choice in how you handled the situation and you made the wrong one."

"I was in the middle of something *very* important. I don't see what else I could have done."

"You could have come out and joined the party for a few minutes. You could have taken a moment to congratulate Miranda on her stellar sales results and then returned to what you were doing. As important as it was, I can't imagine that taking just a few minutes out of your day to thank Miranda would have killed you. And the gesture would have meant a lot to her. Instead, you chose to spend that same amount of time yelling at people and slamming doors. I don't think that kind of behavior casts the right shadow."

"Well, I guess we're just going to have to disagree about this because I really don't see it that way."

Jeff was starting to feel as if he were talking to a wall. It was becoming clear that Adam wasn't going to take responsibility for his actions unless forced to. Jeff didn't like giving people ultimatums, but he liked even less the idea of backing down from something this important. He believed that any employee, regardless of his or her position, who didn't live up to or undermined the company's values simply had to go. Jeff knew that even one bad attitude could spread like a cancer though an organization. Adam had been with the company for a long time and he was very good at what he did, but no one was indispensable.

At the same time, Jeff also believed that people deserved an opportunity to change before being shown the door. So he said to Adam, "I don't want to beat around the bush here. If you want to continue to work for this company, you need to change the way you deal with people, and you need to start doing that right now. That means no more yelling at people who are being celebrated. That means no more shutting down conversations during meetings. And most of all, that means taking an active part in creating a spirit of recognition and an environment where all people are respected and appreciated, one where we celebrate anyone who performs above expectations. My question to you is: Do you think you can do that?"

Jeff could see that Adam was fuming now. He looked as if he had been backed into a corner and he wasn't happy about it. He stared at Jeff for an uncomfortable moment or two without saying a word. Then, through gritted teeth, he said, "Jeff, I've been at this for nearly forty years, and I'm not about to start throwing confetti now. It's just not what I do."

Jeff let out a long, slow breath. Adam wasn't going to come around no matter how many chances he was given. He was making that crystal clear. And that meant there was only one thing Jeff could do.

"If that's the case, Adam, then it's time for you to leave this company."

Chapter 18

As soon as Jeff got back to his office, he had Marjorie call an emergency team meeting so he could get ahead of the news. It was unfortunate what had happened, but Jeff decided that if he explained it in the right way, then he could use Adam's exit as an example of his expectations for the rest of the team. The last thing he wanted was for them to think he couldn't hold people accountable just because he was leading the charge on recognition. This would be a good opportunity to point out the importance of recognizing both the good *and* the bad in the company, what works and what doesn't. And when something doesn't work, you have to do something about it. If that meant some people had to lose their jobs, then that was just the way it was.

When Jeff walked into the conference room about forty minutes later, he was pleased to see everyone chatting easily with one another. Anna was telling the group about her recognition award, and they were enthusiastically asking her questions about it. They clearly hadn't heard yet about what had happened with Adam.

"Thanks for coming on such short notice," Jeff said as he walked in. "Have a seat and we'll get this done quickly so you can get back to what you were doing."

"Shouldn't we wait for Adam?" Dan asked.

"Well, that's what I need to talk to you about," Jeff answered. The tenor of the room changed abruptly at Jeff's remark. Everyone was now looking at him anxiously.

"I'm afraid that Adam is no longer working with us."

There was a pause as the news sank in. It was Nicole who finally asked, "What happened?"

"Adam told me in no uncertain terms that he didn't wish to take part in the changes that are now taking place. I told him that if that was the case, then it wasn't possible for him to stay. And he didn't disagree. It's unfortunate that we're losing him, but that's the way it has to be. We are a team and we have to stand together. There's simply no other way to make this company work."

Jeff paused for a moment to gauge the reaction of his team members. Everyone looked a little uncomfortable about the news, but no one seemed surprised. They knew what Adam was like, and they knew he didn't think much of Jeff's ideas about recognition. In fact, they probably knew it better than Jeff himself because they had worked with Adam longer. They hadn't seen *this* coming exactly, but a confrontation had seemed inevitable.

"I wanted to tell you the news before any rumors started flying," Jeff continued. "I also wanted to give you all a chance to talk it through and ask me anything that's on your mind. Those are the main reasons why I called this emergency meeting. But I also want you to know that I'm particularly sorry to have to deliver this news to you now. I had been hoping that our next meeting would be more of a celebration of all your efforts. I've been really impressed by how you've created meaningful experiences for the people in your departments. Now is not the right time, but when we get together next week, I'd like to have a celebration of our own to talk about the great things you've been doing to recognize your people and figure out how we can take it to the next level."

"I think that's a great idea." Much to Jeff's pleasure, it was Anna who said it, but the others nodded in agreement.

"All right. Does anyone have any questions? There are no secrets here, so if anything is bothering you, I want to hear about it."

"I have one question," Nicole said. "What are we going to do about filling the hole that Adam is leaving behind?"

"This just happened less than an hour ago, so there's no plan in place yet, but we'll figure that out together,"

Jeff responded. "I really appreciate any help any of you can offer as we make our way through this transition."

Everyone accepted Jeff's answer and, as there were no more questions, Jeff let them go. As the last person departed the room, he breathed a huge sigh of relief. He had been worried that Adam's departure might set them back just when they were finally starting to move forward. Fortunately, they had all taken the news well. And losing someone who was so obviously against what he was trying to do was only likely to reinforce his vision even further. After all, anyone who had been holding on to doubts that recognition was his top priority couldn't possibly have them now.

Jeff knew, however, that there could still be some among his team members who were silently wondering whether focusing on recognition would actually produce results. In that regard, Jeff still had a lot to prove to everyone, including himself.

Chapter 19

Later that same day, Jeff received an unexpected visit from Dan. Jeff knew Dan and Adam had been friendly, so he was starting to wonder whether in less than a day, he was about to lose his second employee. His COO, looking unsure of himself, entered his office and sat down. Jeff had his reservations about Dan, but he was hoping to be proved wrong.

"I wanted to talk to you about Adam," Dan began.

"Of course," Jeff answered. "What's on your mind?"

"Before the meeting, Manuel and Nicole, even Anna, were talking about their recognition events during the past week. When you walked in, I was already feeling a bit guilty that I hadn't done anything myself to bring recognition to the operations department. Then I heard the news about Adam . . ."

"And?" Jeff had a feeling he knew where this was going, and it wasn't what he'd initially thought. Still, he wasn't going to make this too easy on Dan.

"Well, Adam was sort of my mentor here. I've always followed his lead more or less. But it seems like doing that this time . . . well, it seems like it might have been a mistake."

"Why is that?"

"Well, I guess I want you to know, I really like working here. And I'm sorry that I haven't done more to support the changes you are trying to bring to the organization."

"I'm glad to hear that, Dan, but I have to ask, what's been the holdup?"

"I don't know. Adam didn't think your ideas would . . . stick, I guess. But I'm starting to realize that Adam wasn't right about everything."

"I certainly believe he was wrong about this."

"The thing is, I was really surprised by what happened in Cleveland. I mean, *really*. When you introduced the idea of recognition, with the jar your grandkid made you and reminding us all to say thank you to people, I guess it sounded to me more like the kind of lessons my kids are learning in grade school rather than something revolutionary enough to turn this company around. I mean, it's all kind of common sense. Not that I'm knocking it, it's just . . ."

"I think I know what you mean, Dan. These ideas really are common sense in a way. But it makes me think of something my grandfather used to say. He obviously built a great company, and he became a pretty wise man along the way. He always had great insights and a great way of putting things. One of his favorite pearls was 'The problem with common sense is it's not all that common.' I remembered that when I got here and saw how things worked. The ideas I proposed about recognition and using it to drive results may be common sense, but it was completely absent from the environment here as far as I could tell."

"I guess words are different from deeds. It all sounded a bit, well, silly when you first described it. But then it was pretty amazing how everyone reacted to Bob when he got his award. No one seemed jealous or to think it was silly. In fact, they all seemed inspired by the moment."

"That's exactly the kind of feeling I want to bring to this place, and not just once in a while. I want that spirit to be alive throughout every corner of this company each and every day."

"I'm starting to get that now. Even Anna seemed jazzed this morning, and that's not her typical mood at meetings," Dan grinned.

"I appreciate you being honest with me about this, but I also have to tell you," Jeff said, not wanting to let him laugh off what had happened, "I'm going to need to see more from you. As the person in charge of both operations and HR, you have more people under you than anyone else, and yet you're the only person on the leadership team who hasn't done something to bring recognition to his department. I need you to step up and make this happen quickly. We have no time to waste."

Jeff and Dan continued talking for a little while after that. By the time Dan left, Jeff was feeling cautiously optimistic about his COO. Dan had promised to step up his game, and Jeff had told him he'd be watching to see what kind of impact he could have on his department. He still had reservations about Dan's leadership abilities, but he was willing to give him the benefit of the doubt . . . for now.

Later that evening, after Marjorie had gone home and the office was quiet, Jeff sat in silence contemplating his tumultuous day. It had been the most eventful one he'd had so far at Happy Face Toys, but that didn't strike him as a bad thing. The company had needed some shaking up after all, and that's exactly what had happened. In recent days he'd had some uncomfortable run-ins, lost a key team member, and there was still a ton of work to do. It wasn't going to be easy, but it finally felt as if he were surrounded by people who understood his vision and were willing to follow his lead. Now all he needed to worry about was whether his ideas would have the kind of impact he was hoping for—because if people didn't see results soon, he knew they wouldn't follow him for long.

PART III

OGO in Action

Chapter 20

The following week, Jeff was in his office on Monday morning preparing for his weekly executive team meeting. He was proud of the way his team members had started to embrace recognition and make it their own, but he knew it wasn't enough. Just because they'd had some breakthroughs didn't mean they could rest on their laurels. In fact, he felt it was time to take things to the next level. He needed to push his team even harder and get many more people involved before recognition could become a catalyst for the kind of results the company so badly needed. That was his objective for their team meeting that morning, and Jeff was hoping that instead of pushing back, the entire team would be eager to see how far they could take things.

When his executive team had gathered in the conference room, Jeff set the stage in the same way he had when he first introduced the idea of recognition to them.

"We have a huge challenge ahead of us. Our sales, as

you know, are down seven percent. Worse yet, they've been down for five straight years in a row, so our profits are in even worse shape. We need to turn the company around so that instead of losing ground year after year, we can start growing again. That's something we all want to see happen. That's something we all *need* to see happen." Jeff saw heads nodding in agreement as he said this. So far so good.

"Unfortunately, what we've been doing hasn't been working. The talent in this room, as good as it is, is just not enough to get us where we need to go. We need the talents of the *whole organization,* and that means that every single person who works for Happy Face Toys must be motivated and working together toward the same goal: to put this company back on a path to growth. How do we start doing that?"

Jeff paused, hoping someone in the room would help him out. He wasn't disappointed.

"We've got to fire up our people by recognizing the behaviors and actions that will turn this business around once and for all," Nicole chimed in with enthusiasm. Again, the others around the table nodded in agreement.

"Thanks, Nicole," Jeff said, beaming at her. "I couldn't have said that any better."

Jeff was anxious to move on and start doing what needed to be done to get those results, but he didn't want to move on too quickly. If there were still holdouts in the room, he needed those people to speak up *now*. So he continued.

"What I need to know is whether everyone in this room is fully on board with what I'm trying to do. In order to make recognition work on the scale I'm envisioning, every single one of you has to do more than just buy into it. You need to champion it. You need to talk about it as often as you can. You need to practice it regularly and enthusiastically. You need to make sure *all* of the people working under you know what it's all about, and that *they're* making sure the people who work under *them* get it too. You need to inspire as many people as you can so that they'll be moved to inspire even more people. I call this the exponential power of giving. When you give recognition to others and help them reach their potential, then they become motivated to do the same. It creates a ripple effect, and it's how we can build an organization where the whole is greater than the sum of its parts. It's how we can build the kind of powerful organization that can tackle whatever challenges come our way."

Jeff knew he was laying it on thick. He knew he was asking a lot from them, but he truly believed in what he was saying. He believed in the notion that a rising tide lifts all ships. He believed this was the best way for *all* of them to succeed and, as a result, for the company itself to succeed. He hoped they believed it too. And so far no one was taking him on.

"Your role in this is essential," Jeff continued, "so before we move forward, I need to hear from each and every one of you that you're fully on board and willing to do what it takes."

Jeff stopped speaking and waited, taking in each member of his team one by one.

Manuel was the first to speak up. "I know I was a bit slow at first, and I'm sorry about that, but I'm fully on board now. You can count on me."

"Me too," Nicole added. "What's more, I'm looking forward to it."

Jeff smiled and was about to thank Nicole for her enthusiasm when Dan chimed in. "I'm in too," he said. Jeff wondered for a brief moment whether Dan was jumping on the bandwagon because everyone else was, but because he had no specific reason to doubt him, he let the thought go.

Jeff then looked at the one remaining team member. Anna hadn't said anything yet, so Jeff addressed her directly. No one was going to fly under the radar on this one. It was just too important for that.

"Anna," he said looking her in the eye, "what about you?" Anna looked back at him evenly, and Jeff wasn't sure how she was going to respond.

"I know I doubted you in the beginning," she began,

carefully choosing her words, "but that was then. I've seen how this works, I've seen recognition in action, and I now know my people can get a lot out of it. I now know I can get a lot out of it too. So you can definitely count me in," she said with a smile.

Jeff didn't let his team see it, but he breathed a sigh of relief. Then he looked at them all, and his excitement started to build. It was really amazing to see the light-bulbs going on and to think about how far they'd come together. This really felt like *his* team for the first time since he'd arrived at Happy Face, and he didn't want the moment to pass without comment. So he said to them: "Thank you, all of you, for supporting me on this. It means a lot. And I'm glad to hear we're all on the same page . . . *finally.*"

Jeff flashed them a grin as he delivered that last word, and the group responded with a laugh.

"But remember, that's just the first step," Jeff continued, "and we've got a long road ahead of us. We're only five leaders and we've got tens of thousands of team members to get on board with us."

It was time for Jeff to once again set the stage for his team and get them thinking about how they could raise the stakes. So he said to them, "We need to make recognition part of how we do business each and every day, in every corner of the company, all around the globe. What

I want us to focus on today is this: How can we achieve that in the least amount of time?"

No one said anything right away, but that was OK with Jeff. He wanted to push his team out of their comfort zone once again and help them fully appreciate the magnitude of the task before them. So he let them think for a few moments before he offered up an idea.

"Unless anyone has a better idea, I think the first thing we need to do is come up with some guidelines. Some simple principles we can share with the whole organization to explain what we mean when we use the word 'recognition.' Does that sound like a good place to start?"

"You mean like the safety guidelines we have in our factories or like our golden rules of customer service?" Dan asked.

"That's exactly what I mean," Jeff said. "A list we can use to quickly teach everyone about recognition and get everyone on the same page. I like to think of the list as our Guiding Principles of Recognition. To work, they have to be easy to understand, they have to support what we're trying to accomplish, and they have to apply universally, meaning they have to resonate just as much with someone in the mail room as they do with everyone in this room. You all saw me practice recognition in Cleveland, and you've all started doing it in your own departments. So think about what has made it really work for you and for the people around you. I want to have a brainstorming session on this in just a minute, but first, there's something else we need to do."

Jeff quickly checked his phone and found what he was looking for: a text from Marjorie saying, "Ready when you are."

Jeff continued, "Recognition is an idea that's meant to inspire the entire company, so I want the entire company represented in this discussion. Right now, due to Adam's departure, there's a big piece of the company missing from this room."

Jeff then invited Dan to join him at the front of the room. During their discussion after Adam's departure, Dan had come up with a suggestion Jeff thought was a good one. Because Dan still seemed to be struggling with making recognition a big idea in his department, Jeff wanted to encourage him now by giving him credit. As Dan stood next to him, Jeff explained to the others what was happening.

"Dan, who often worked closely with Adam in the past, suggested we appoint someone already in the legal department to be their temporary leader. I don't want any of us to get distracted right now, and this will give us time before we have to focus on searching for Adam's replacement.

Dan recommended someone he thought was up to the task. I've met with this person and I agree, but I'd like to hear what all of you think."

"Who is it?" Anna asked, looking skeptical.

Jeff nodded to Dan. "It's Peter," Dan said to the group. "I got to know him well when we created a human resources manual for the entire company. It was a beast of a job and one that no one was exactly excited about, including Adam. He put Peter in charge of managing their end of it because, as he told me, 'Peter's the kind of guy who knows how to rally the troops.' He did exactly that during the course of a difficult and often tedious project. I believe he's the kind of person who will understand what we're trying to do here. And I believe he'll be able to get his department involved in recognition because everyone there really trusts and respects him."

"So, any thoughts on Dan's proposal?" Jeff asked the group.

"I think Peter's a great choice," Nicole volunteered. "Not to be too blunt about it, but Adam was prickly about being disturbed, so I've often gone to Peter when I needed something. He's always been easy to deal with."

"I agree that bringing in someone new right now would be rough on the department," Manuel added. "They're still getting used to Adam's absence. Soon they're going to have to wrap their heads around making our ideas about

132

recognition a priority as well. A new boss on top of that is a lot."

Jeff smiled. It was the first time he'd heard anyone refer to recognition as "our idea" instead of "Jeff's idea" or "that thing Jeff wants us to do." It was a sign of progress.

"So is everyone in agreement that we'll have Peter represent the legal department for the time being?" Jeff looked pointedly at Anna, who had yet to chime in. She nodded her consent.

"Great, then let's bring him in."

Chapter 21

After welcoming Peter to the team, Jeff got down to business.

"So how do we practice recognition at Happy Face Toys? How do we use it to support our mission of 'putting a smile on every child's face' and our goal of putting the company back on a path to growth? What's going to make this work on a large scale? What's going to help us make the concept clear to everyone? Who wants to start?"

Anna was the first to speak up.

"I've got something. When you first introduced the idea and showed us your OGO jar, I have to admit, I didn't like it," she said with a conciliatory smile.

Jeff smiled back and nodded at her to continue. "What really got in my way was when you pulled out those strips of paper and read us all the things your family had written about you. Don't get me wrong, they said some really nice things. The problem was, I just didn't think I could do that. I'm not exactly a touchy-feely person. I can talk about technology all day long, but sentimental stuff like that is not my forte."

Jeff was surprised by this burst of honesty. But then again, Anna was nothing if not brutally honest.

"What really made the difference for me," Anna continued, "was when you told me to make recognition my own. I didn't have to give out an OGO jar if I didn't want to. I just needed to come up with something that was meaningful to me and my people. That's when I came up with the Top Scorer Award, because so many people in my department grew up on video games and still play them today. Everyone loved that award. I mean, I'd love to get an award like that myself."

"I totally agree with you," Nicole told her. "I've been really inspired by all the different ways people have made recognition their own, and we're just getting started. It's a lot more meaningful than just giving out some old plaque month after month."

"So," Jeff said, "what should we call that principle?"

"How about 'Make it personal?'" Anna suggested.

"I like it," Jeff said. He wrote, "Make it personal" on the whiteboard that had been set up at the front of the room. "Congratulations folks, we've got our first Guiding Principle. So what's next?"

That kicked off a lively discussion that lasted nearly

two hours. Some ideas were debated and thrown out, but several others received the unanimous thumbs up. Manuel came up with "Make it fun," explaining that he threw a surprise party to recognize their monthly sales leader because it was not just fun for her, it was fun for the whole group. Getting everyone involved in the celebration had been a great way to spread the concept beyond just the person being rewarded.

"It reminds me of something my grandfather used to say," Jeff said as he wrote "Make it fun" on the whiteboard. "'Take the business seriously but not yourself. My grandfather was a larger-than-life character who accomplished a lot during his lifetime, so the humility of that statement always stuck with me.'"

Nicole came up with two ideas based on the experience of fielding questions from the employees in Cleveland. "I like what we've come up with, but I think we need to back up a bit and start with something that explains the basic reason why recognition matters so much," she began. "Something like 'People won't care about you if you don't care about them.' That's what I saw in Cleveland. They were feeling like the unwanted stepchildren of this company. They didn't think we cared about them anymore, so they stopped caring about the business."

"You're right," Jeff agreed. "That should be Principle Number One."

He wrote, "People won't care about you if you don't care about them" on the whiteboard.

"I also think we need to say something about doing this regularly," she continued. "If we need people to internalize this quickly, we can't wait for annual performance reviews or even monthly meetings to recognize people. We need to start doing this yesterday."

"How about, 'Recognize great work whenever and wherever you see it'?" Manuel offered.

Everyone agreed, and Jeff added it to their whiteboard list.

Next, it was Dan's turn to contribute something. "I'm not quite sure how to turn this into a principle, but as I was just listening to Nicole, I remembered something I noticed about the way she interacted with the people in Cleveland," he said. "She was able to engage them so easily, and I think it came down to the fact that she was so obviously listening to what they had to say with interest and respect. They could just tell what they said mattered to her."

Jeff looked over at Nicole, who was beaming at the compliment.

"I have something written on a Post-it next to my computer," Nicole said. "It's been there for years and I think of it as my words to live by as a leader. It says, 'The best way to show people you care is to listen to them.'"

"That's a good one. It should come right after our Principle Number One: 'People won't care about you if you don't care about them,'" Jeff said, reordering the principles on the whiteboard as he spoke.

The group batted around a few more ideas after that, but pretty soon the energy in the room began to wane. Jeff decided it was time to stop. "So we've come up with five really good principles," he told the team. "I'm sure we'll refine as we go, but I think we've got enough here to start communicating to the rest of the organization what we're trying to do. What does everyone think? Is there anything else we should discuss before we call this meeting to a close?"

Peter had been quiet during most of the meeting, which Jeff didn't blame him for. He was new to the group and new to his role, so it would probably take awhile before he felt entirely comfortable speaking his mind. He had been actively listening throughout the discussion, however, and was quick to offer approval when an idea resonated with him, which Jeff appreciated. But now he was raising his hand to speak.

Jeff smiled at him. "Go ahead, Peter. You can just speak up if you have something to say."

"Great, thanks," Peter began tentatively. "Well, first off I just wanted to say how inspiring this has been. This is going to be pretty different for many of the people in my department, but I think they'll love it once they understand it."

"Thanks Peter, I'm glad to hear it," Jeff said. He thought that was the end of it, but to his surprise, Peter continued.

"I also wanted to suggest another principle if I could."

"Of course," Jeff said, "what is it?"

"Well, it seems to me that one of the big reasons recognition is so important is because it inspires people to *want* to be involved. It inspires them to open up and contribute their ideas. That's something that, unfortunately, we're not so great at in our department. The ideas we follow through on almost always come from the top. But we do have this one legal assistant who always manages to dig up legal precedents from places no one expects. He's a young guy, very junior in our group, but he has a saying that's always resonated with me. He says: 'A great idea is a great idea no matter where it comes from.' When he says it, it's usually because he's taken an idea from a competitor or a business that, on the surface, seems to have nothing in common with ours. That's a great lesson on its own, but I think the saying also applies to people within an organization. A good idea is simply a good idea, no matter who supplies it. It doesn't matter whether it comes from the boss or an assistant, from someone in an office building or on the factory floor. After all, more good ideas are what we're all looking for, right?"

"That's exactly right," Jeff responded, feeling especially glad they had invited Peter to the table. "That was something I tried to explain when I first introduced the concept of recognition, but you've said it better than I ever did or ever could."

Jeff thought for a moment, and then he continued. "I would add that we want not only to recognize that a good idea can come from anyone, no matter what the person's role is, but we also want to celebrate that fact. One thing I've learned over the years is that the higher up you go, the more important it is to celebrate the ideas of others, as much as or even more than your own. That's how you get everyone to *want* to contribute instead of just looking to you as the leader to provide all the ideas and direction. And if we can get more good ideas to come to the surface, then there's no reason we can't solve any of the problems this company faces—now or in the future. If we can harness the combined talents of everyone in our organization, then there's nothing we can't do together. I really believe that."

Jeff turned to Peter and said, "Thank you for contributing your ideas. I want everyone working toward making this place better. It's essential to what we're doing here."

Jeff turned and wrote on the whiteboard: "A great idea can come from anywhere." As he did so, he felt a surge of confidence that the team was moving in the right direction. And boy did it feel good.

Chapter 22

After the meeting, Jeff returned to his office, where he spent the next hour looking at the list of Guiding Principles, reordering them, filling in an explanation for each, and playing with the wording. When he'd refined it as much as he could, he called Marjorie and asked her to join him in his office when she had a moment.

"What can I do for you?" Marjorie asked, sitting down across from him.

"I want to know what you think about this," Jeff said, handing her a sheet of paper. On it, he'd written:

Recognition Is Our Way Forward
Guiding Principles for the Happy Face Toy
Company

Principle #1: People won't care about you if you don't care about them—you have to show people you care about them before you can expect any-thing from them.

Principle #2: The best way to show people you care is to listen to them—people won't believe you care about them if you don't take the time to hear and acknowledge what they have to say. Besides, you can safely assume that everyone knows some-thing you don't, so everyone is worth listening to.

Principle #3: A great idea can come from anywhere—great ideas don't always come from the highest-ranking or most experienced person in the room. In fact, most of the time they don't. But great ideas are essential to the success of any organization, so they need to be sought out and supported. A good idea is simply a good idea no matter where it comes from, so view everyone as a potential source.

Principle #4: Recognize great work and great ideas whenever and wherever you see them—great leaders celebrate other people's ideas as much, or even more than, their own, and they do it in a way that's spontaneous, real, and from the heart. In fact, the more spontaneous you are, the better. Don't wait for monthly meetings or annual performance reviews to show people you appreciate the work they do or believe in an idea they've come up with. Opportunities to recognize good work happen all the time, so look for those opportunities and make them count.

Principle #5: Make recognition fun—everyone will want to be involved in recognition if you create shared experiences that are fun for everyone, and not just for the person being recognized.

Principle #6: Make it personal—that is, make it personal to you *and* the person you're recognizing. Don't just give out the typical certificate or plaque when you recognize someone's contributions. Putting your personal stamp on the award you give makes it more meaningful, memorable, and fun for you and for those around you. And make sure to personalize each award by being specific about what that person has done to earn it!

Jeff watched Marjorie's face closely as she took a few moments to read through what he had written. She kept her expression even as she read, but when she finished, she looked up at Jeff with a big smile on her face.

"You came up with these?" she asked.

"The whole team came up with them together. That was what we did during our meeting this morning."

"Well, I think it's great," she told him handing the sheet back to him, and she clearly meant it.

"Anything you would change?"

"No, there's nothing I would change about what's on the page, but I do have a question for you."

"And what's that?" Jeff asked

"How are you going to get the ideas off the page?"

"What do you mean?"

"Well, those are really great words. They strike a chord and they have a powerful message behind them. But it seems to me that the real trick is going to be turning those words into actions. How are you going to make everyone understand that this is really the way forward and not just another missive from headquarters that they'll read today and forget tomorrow?"

"That is going to be tricky," Jeff agreed. "I thought I'd send out a personal email to each and every employee telling them that recognition is my top priority and including a list of these principles that they can print out and put up on their office wall or post in the lounge or the break room or wherever."

"That's a good start," Marjorie said. "What else?"

"Well, Anna's team has finished setting up the new communication system linking all the people in all our locations around the world. I could use that to do a webcast where I explain the principles in more detail and maybe take some questions from people."

"Good, and what else?" Marjorie prompted.

"You think I need to do more than that?"

"What I think is that I've been working for people in positions of authority for a long time. I've seen leaders introduce all sorts of new ideas, some of which worked and some of which didn't. It seems to me that the difference between something working and not working, at least in the beginning, before you have a chance to see any effects, really comes down to how much that leader gets behind it. If you want recognition to be a big deal, then *you* have to make a big deal about it."

"You're right," Jeff said. The magnitude of what still needed to be done was bigger than even he'd realized. "Any ideas?"

"Put your money where your mouth is. Start by 'Making it fun.' Throw a party for everyone here at headquarters to introduce the concept."

"That's a good idea. We can certainly do that."

"And then take it on the road. Do exactly the same thing in all our locations."

"You mean introduce it myself?"

"Yes," Marjorie said.

"At *all* our locations?"

"Yes," Marjorie said again. "If you want to get people at every one of our locations involved, then I think you should go to every one of our locations yourself."

Jeff thought about that for a moment. On the one hand, Marjorie was right. If he really wanted people to understand how important this was to him, he needed to do more than just send out a company-wide email blast to show them. On the other hand, there was still so much to do here in Chicago. Could he really afford to take time away from the office when their numbers were still so dismal? He wasn't so sure that he could.

"Let's get started on that email message to all our employees, and let's set up a party for the whole office here in Chicago. Everyone's invited, from the janitors on up to senior staff. Then we'll go from there," Jeff said, unable to commit to more than that right now.

"OK, we'll start there, but keep in mind what I said," Marjorie cautioned. "I just think there's no substitute for the power of asking people personally for their help. Or for explaining to them yourself why you believe it's so important."

Jeff knew instinctively that Marjorie was probably

right, but whether he could really follow through on it was a different question. He just wasn't sure he had the time or the energy to do *everything* she was suggesting. At least not until the company's numbers started turning around.

Chapter 23

With Marjorie's help, Jeff quickly organized what they called their Recognition Is Our Way Forward event as a first step toward introducing recognition to the larger organization. To show everyone just how important he believed this was, he shut down the Chicago office for an entire afternoon, suspending all work and even asking everyone to avoid checking email. Every single employee, from the executive team to the mail room, was asked to join him in the auditorium instead.

Jeff kicked things off with a presentation, during which he introduced his OGO Award and the Guiding Principles of Recognition, and fielded questions from anyone who had one about what they were trying to do and why. Afterward, he invited everyone to continue discussing the topic over pizza and drinks. He brought in a "recognition band" to play music and rally the troops. He even set up a poster board spanning an entire wall in the auditorium, on which people were invited to write thank-you messages to anyone they wanted, for any reason whatsoever. People really got into it, even standing on chairs to write more messages when the space below got too crowded.

The event had felt like a genuine celebration. Since then Jeff had been receiving great feedback about recognition, and not just from his executive team. All sorts of employees from different parts of the company had come by his office or stopped him in the hallways to tell him about their experiences with recognition—either giving or receiving or even just witnessing it. Jeff was impressed by how people were really taking the "Make it fun" and "Make it personal" principles to heart. A trend seemed to have developed, probably inspired by Anna's Top Scorer Award, that Jeff hadn't anticipated. Many of the awards that people came up with made use of classic toys from the company's own product lines. A leader in the product development department, for example, created the Spaceship Award, a 1950s-era mechanical spaceship that was awarded for "giving liftoff to new ideas." Someone in Manuel's department had given out the Bubble Machine Award, a soap bubble machine for "bursting the barriers that get in the way of our success." Manuel had walked in on his team's celebration and witnessed the entire group scrambling about and laughing like a bunch of kids as they tried to pop as many bubbles as they could before the machine ran out of soap. Jeff was proud to say he never could have come up with so many entertaining ideas all on his own.

From what Jeff was seeing and hearing, his vision for making recognition a way of life for the people at Happy Face Toys was really starting to take hold. Unfortunately, not everything was going so great on other fronts. About a week after their officewide celebration, Marjorie popped her head into Jeff's office to announce a visit that Jeff had been dreading. It was Nicole, and she had brought with her the company's most recent numbers.

"Give me the headlines," Jeff said to her as they both took their seats.

Nicole chewed on her lip for a moment and then said, "Well, I guess what it boils down to is that the news is not as bad as usual. Our sales are still declining, but profits haven't declined quite as much overall in the recent quarter, mostly due to a reduction in expenditures."

Nicole was trying to put a positive spin on it, but Jeff didn't want to kid himself. This wasn't good news. Of course he'd seen it coming. It wasn't as if he'd expected miracles this early in the game. He knew it would take time for recognition to kick in and lead to results, but it was still sobering to see the company's poor performance in black and white. And soon he was going to have to face the board of directors with these results, which was something he wasn't looking forward to at all.

"All right," he said, pulling himself together. "Let's figure out how we're going to present this to the board while making it clear that we don't expect the bad news to continue forever."

Nicole and Jeff put their heads together and worked nonstop for more than an hour. They were still deep in discussion when a commotion outside interrupted them. "What's that?" Nicole asked.

"I don't know. I'm sure it will go away soon," Jeff replied, trying to ignore it and pick up where they'd left off.

But the noise didn't go away. In fact, it grew louder. Pretty soon they could hear people clapping and cheering and stomping their feet. Jeff couldn't concentrate, so he called out to Marjorie, "What's all that noise about?"

"It's a party to celebrate someone in marketing," Marjorie responded. "I'm not sure what for. Do you want me to find out?"

"No," Jeff called back. Then he turned to Nicole. "Maybe we should take this to your office." He was suddenly feeling that he understood Adam a little better. Not that he thought the former CLO's departure was a mistake, but he understood how hard it must have been for Adam to sit at his desk and listen to all the noise when he was trying to get something done. Jeff was having trouble resisting the urge to go out to the hallway and ask everyone to be quiet himself, so he figured the best thing he could do was get away from it all.

"Actually, Jeff," Nicole said gently, "don't you think we ought to go out there and join them?"

"No, not today. There just isn't time," Jeff said firmly. The truth was that he really just didn't feel like it.

"But it will only take a few minutes," Nicole persisted. "Besides, we could probably use a break."

"No, I don't need a break. What I need to do is get through all this," Jeff said, gesturing to the mess of papers in front of them.

"But Jeff," Nicole said a little more forcefully now, "what about the shadow of the leader?"

Jeff let out a slow breath. And then he started laughing. "You're right. Of course you're right. That's the problem with going public with your ideas," he said wryly. "As soon as you fail to live up to them, there's always someone there to point out the error of your ways."

Nicole smiled at him. "I believe you actually think that's a *good* thing, not a problem."

"I do, of course, but that doesn't mean it's always so easy to take."

Nicole gave him a quick pat on the back, and the two of them went out into the hallway to join the celebration.

After a few minutes of cheers and congratulations, Jeff actually felt better. He was glad Nicole had insisted they join in, but in the back of his mind he was also wondering how he could possibly keep everything going. The company was in the tank, and the board of directors wasn't going to be happy about it, especially because he had decided against some of their recommendations in recent weeks. If he couldn't start showing them results soon, he knew they were going to lose confidence in him. Happy Face Toys needed new ideas, and they needed them now. Otherwise Jeff might just go down in history as that clueless leader who was handing out OGO jars as the company went down in flames.

Chapter 24

"Ready to face the music?" Nicole asked half jokingly as she appeared in the doorway of Jeff's office. It was time for their quarterly board meeting, and as much time as they had spent preparing for it, he still wasn't sure what he might be facing once he got into that room.

This was the first time Jeff would come face to face with his board of directors since he'd taken over as CEO. The last time he'd met with them was when he'd twisted their arms just enough to give him the job. He knew they were still wary of him, and he figured he might be in for a bit of a beating because of the company's most recent results. But Jeff had only been CEO for one business quarter. The board was filled with seasoned business executives who understood quite well that a company of this size didn't shift dramatically overnight. But that didn't mean they were going to be easy on Jeff when they saw their more recent sales figures.

Jeff joined Nicole, who gave him an encouraging smile, and together they walked silently to the conference room.

"Well, here's our brand-new CEO," one of the board members, Art Selby, said, clapping Jeff on the back as he entered the room. "I'm looking forward to hearing what you've got for us today."

Jeff winced internally, both because of Art's overly enthusiastic pat on the back and because his words seemed tinged with sarcasm. Just a few months before, Art had been the loudest and most adamant opponent of Jeff's bid to become CEO, so Jeff doubted that Art was really looking forward to anything he had to say.

"Thanks, Art," Jeff responded coolly, "that's all I can ask for." Jeff decided he'd better leave it at that rather than risk saying something he'd regret. So he excused himself, walked to the head of the table, and busied himself with setting up his laptop for the presentation to come.

A few minutes later, everyone was seated and ready to start. Besides Nicole and himself, in attendance were eight other executives representing a wide variety of industries, from construction to health care to consumer products, including Art, who had once headed up one of the country's largest investment firms.

"Thank you for coming today," Jeff began. "I'm going to start this meeting in the same way that I start all my meetings with our executive team: by defining the harsh reality of our company's situation. Every week I remind my team that we're facing a huge challenge. As you know, our sales are down seven percent. Worse yet, they've been down for five straight years in a row, so our profits are in even worse shape. This past quarter wasn't much different. You all have our quarterly report in front of you so you can see this for yourselves."

A few board members opened up their reports and started scanning them, but most were still fixated on Jeff. So Jeff continued.

"The question, of course, is the same one that's been on the table since I took this job, which is, what am *I* going to do to turn this company around. You gave me a year to show you something, and believe me, I've felt the pressure of that ticking clock every single day since I got here. So let me tell you a little bit about what I've been doing to get this company back on track."

Jeff then took the board members through a slide presentation he had created with the help of Marjorie and Nicole. One slide showed his OGO Award, and Jeff told them exactly what it was and where it had come from. Another showed a picture of Bob receiving the award, which gave Jeff a chance to tell them Bob's story. More slides showed the different ways people were being recognized throughout the organization for different contributions to the company. And a final slide showed their

Guiding Principles of Recognition. After going through them one by one, Jeff said to the group, "This is what we're going to use to cascade recognition throughout every corner of the Happy Face Toy Company. It's through recognizing the ideas and behaviors we need that we're going to drive results and turn this company around. My goal is nothing short of making this company an industry leader once again. That's going to require some radical changes in how we do business, but I believe we've finally got a plan that can work and that our people can get behind. And we're off to a solid start."

With that, Jeff closed his laptop. Before he even got a chance to ask if there were any questions, Art was already on the edge of his seat.

"Excuse me, Jeff, but a little birdie told me you'd decided against shutting down the Cleveland plant. Why is that?"

Jeff wondered briefly who that little birdie was. He suspected it was his former CLO, but it really didn't matter. The information was true and the question was fair enough.

"That's correct," Jeff said. "I visited the plant, more than once, and I believe they still have a lot to offer. In fact, their biggest problem, in my view, is that they haven't been getting enough support from our main office. Once they get that, I believe they'll surprise us. So I've decided to hold off on closing the plant for at least the year, and we'll see if, with the right support, they can turn around their performance during that time."

"Do you think you have that much time to give them?" The question came from Jennifer Williams, CEO of a large food and beverage company. She wasn't asking with the same smirk that Art had shown, but she did sound concerned.

"Honestly, Jennifer, I don't think I have much choice. Shutting them down may save us some money in the short term, but it's not going to give us the kind of long-term results the company needs. That's a much more complex issue that stems from what I see as a fundamental problem with how this business has been run in recent years. I'm looking to make big changes, but I know that change doesn't happen overnight. Believe me when I tell you we're working hard to speed up the clock each and every day."

Jennifer seemed satisfied with that, at least for the moment, but Greg Washington, a veteran of the construction industry, had a different question. "Are you seeing signs that your people are receptive to this new approach?" he asked with genuine curiosity.

Nicole jumped in to field that one, and Jeff was immensely grateful for the break. He smiled as he listened to her tell the board about some of the things she'd witnessed during her visit to Cleveland, during their launch party in

Chicago, and within her own department, where she'd instituted her own version of Jeff's OGO Award. "In short," Nicole told them, "the answer to your question is that people have been more than receptive to this approach. I think they've really been longing for something like this for quite some time."

"I know what you mean," Greg responded with a sympathy that surprised Jeff. "Not long ago, when the real estate business was in the dumps, we had a really hard time motivating our people to hang in there with us. Rallying your people when things are great and you can promise them a big bonus at the end of the year, well that's easy. But believe me, I know how hard it is when things are rough. And things are certainly pretty rough right now at Happy Face."

Jeff appreciated the show of support, but Art wasn't ready to let him off the hook.

"It's all well and good that your people are feeling better about themselves," he sneered, "but you just got through showing us yet another dismal earnings report. Forgive me if I don't see how all this feel-good stuff translates into hard and fast results. At the end of the day, it's those results that we need to see."

Jeff took a breath and steadied himself. He'd expected these kinds of questions, but Art still rubbed him the wrong way.

"I'm well aware of that," Jeff began slowly, "but what you might be missing in all this is that it's our people who are going to deliver those results. We can't do it without them. So we need to focus on giving them more of what they need, so they can drive the results the company needs."

"And what makes you so sure this recognition thing is going to motivate people to give you those results?"

"Well, it's not as if I have a crystal ball. No one can see the future, but I have seen how people have responded so far. And we're just getting started. What's more, I believe this approach is not just what's right for this business; it's also the right thing to do. Period. Every single person on this planet deserves to feel valued for what they contribute. My grandfather taught me that. He always said to me, 'Do the right thing and the right thing will happen.' We haven't been treating people right here at Happy Face Toys, and it shows."

"With all due respect, Jeff, your grandfather has been gone for quite some time now. The world has changed since his day."

Jeff winced. "With all due respect to you, Art, some things don't change. Like an individual's desire to be appreciated. That's pretty universal. And I think everyone in this room has enough experience to agree on that."

Art was looking skeptically at him, but he didn't disagree. So Jeff continued.

"Besides, if it weren't for my grandfather and his views on how to fire up his people, none of us would be sitting here right now debating this topic. So before you dismiss my ideas out of hand, how about you just give me a chance—a real chance, not just one quarterly earnings report—to show you what I can do. After all, wasn't that what we agreed to the last time we were sitting here together?"

Art looked as if he were about to say something, but Jennifer jumped in, clearly looking to head Art off before the confrontation could get out of hand.

"You're right, Jeff," she said. "I think you've shown us something here today, but the proof is in the pudding, as they say. If you're really on to something, then we'll see it reflected in the results soon enough."

Chapter 25

The message the board of directors had left Jeff with was as clear as night and day: he was getting a pass for now because they understood that change takes time, but he was also on a short leash. Give it another quarter or two and they expected to see some real progress.

Because only Nicole had attended the board meeting with him, Jeff updated the rest of the executive team on what had happened during their next weekly meeting. After reviewing with them the previous quarter's disappointing numbers, he asked every one of his key leaders to make a special point of using recognition to promote the creation and adoption of innovative new ideas. They needed new products, new processes, and new efficiencies that would help them make a dent in their dismal bottom line, and they needed them now.

"Jeff, I have to tell you, I'm not exactly sure how you

see us using recognition to do that," Dan admitted after Jeff had communicated this challenge.

"Well, give me an instance of how you've been using recognition lately in your department," Jeff responded, hoping to show Dan what he meant through a real-world example.

"I came up with what I think is a pretty personal and meaningful award. It's my Ace Navigator Award, which is a remote-controlled airplane given for 'deftly navigating stormy weather and helping the team soar.' I gave it to the guy in logistics who finally fixed Cleveland's absent driver problem. I talked to Doug over there a couple of weeks ago, and he assured me there are no more trucks just sitting on the lot with no one to drive them."

"That's great. I'm really glad to hear it. And I'm really glad you've used recognition to underscore the importance of solving problems like that one. When you're looking for the next person to give your award to, think about rewarding innovation. Find someone who has come up with a great new idea or a new way of looking at something and then let everyone else know that's why this person is being recognized."

Dan nodded, but Jeff had a feeling he shouldn't stop there. He didn't want Dan to just go off and do exactly what he'd suggested. He wanted Dan to use that as an example and start thinking this way for himself. Besides, he'd already heard about Dan's Ace Navigator Award. He wanted to know what else he'd come up with. So he asked Dan, "What else have you done to bring a spirit of recognition to the people in HR and operations?"

"Well, after I gave the award, I sent out an email report telling everyone in my department about it. I thought that would inspire them to come up with their own awards for their own groups."

"OK," Jeff was starting to get concerned. "And what else?"

"What else?"

"Yes, didn't you give out that award weeks ago?"

"I did, but . . . well."

Dan stopped talking then and looked guiltily at Jeff. It was clear he hadn't done anything else to try to fire up his people.

Jeff just stood there shaking his head for a moment. How had this happened? Hadn't he *just* had a conversation with Dan about stepping up his game? He had to wonder if Dan was really trying at all. But rather than get upset at him, he decided to use the moment.

"Dan, you preside over the largest department in our organization. Are you telling me that in nearly a month's time, no one in your group has done anything that deserves to be recognized?"

"Well, I guess they must have."

"And don't you think it's your job to make yourself aware of such things?"

Dan nodded at him. Jeff could tell he was feeling embarrassed and he didn't want to discourage him, so he added something to soften the blow.

"I really appreciate what you've tried to do so far, but in the future I need you to be really diligent about *continually* making recognition a priority in your department. What I suggest, to you and to everyone in this room, is that you print out our Guiding Principles and post them prominently on your wall. Look at them every day and ask yourself two questions: What can *I* do to promote these principles? And how can *I* use these principles to promote the mission and goals of the company? Always remember, if you don't care, neither will anyone else."

Dan didn't say much after that and soon the meeting came to a close. As Jeff walked back to his office, he found himself still wondering about his head of operations. He wasn't sure whether Dan fully understood what they were trying to do, or if he was still waiting to see if Jeff and his guiding principles were going to stick around before he put too much effort into it. In the end, Jeff decided he would replace Dan if he had to, but he really didn't want to lose another team member just now. Besides, he saw potential in Dan. He decided his strategy would be to give him as much direct feedback as possible to make sure he was casting the right shadow as a leader, and then fire him only if he still didn't step up to the plate. He would leave the choice up to Dan.

Jeff also decided he needed to take what had happened as a lesson for himself. He needed to step up his own accountability. It wasn't enough to just tell people once or twice what he wanted from them and expect them to fully understand or accept it. He needed to keep reinforcing his message until it became almost second nature, until everyone knew what he was going to say before he said it. That was how he could make sure everyone understood just how important it was.

One thing was certain, if a member of his own leadership team was still unclear about how important recognition was and how to use it effectively, then surely people were unclear about it elsewhere in the company too. Marjorie had been right when she'd suggested he couldn't just rely on emails or webcasts to spread the world. He needed to take responsibility himself, just as he'd challenged Dan to do. He needed to get as many people involved as he could. He needed as many ambassadors for recognition as he could find.

By the time Jeff got back to his office, he'd made a decision, one that he immediately revealed to his assistant.

"Marjorie," he said to her when he walked in the door, "you were right."

"Glad to hear it," Marjorie said, looking up from her computer screen. "What about?"

"About the right way to introduce recognition."

Marjorie smiled at him. "Go on," she said.

"Ever since our talk, I've been trying to figure out an easier way to roll out recognition to the entire organization. But I've finally come to the conclusion that if I want to cast the right kind of shadow as a leader, I can't take the easy way out. I need to *show* everyone at Happy Face that recognizing their good work is my top priority.

"And what does that mean exactly?" Marjorie asked.

"It means we need to plan a trip. It's time for me to take my ideas on the road."

Chapter 26

Over the next several weeks Jeff visited Happy Face locations across the United States and abroad, from South Carolina to Shanghai and many, many places in between. Everywhere he went he introduced recognition in the same way he had for his own team. He showed everyone his OGO jar, explained where it came from, and told them the story about Bob. Then he said:

"I never want there to be another Bob in this organization again. I never want there to be someone who has contributed so much to the company without realizing how much the company appreciates them in return. I want everyone to know how much we value them and their work. Every person, no matter what they do, no matter how old or young, no matter how junior or senior, *everyone* deserves to be appreciated for their contributions. That idea is crucial to the success of this company. Why? Because it is not going to succeed or fail based on the contributions of any one of us—not even the CEO. No one in this world can succeed alone. We need everyone working together to make something *big* happen at the Happy Face Toy Company."

Everywhere he traveled Jeff's speech really seemed to resonate with a lot of people, but that didn't mean he could call his trip an all-out success. The truth was that reactions were mixed, and there were more than a few bumps along the way to introducing recognition to his team members around the globe.

One of his first international stops was at the European Sales Center in England, where he met with the division's director, Stephen. Stephen's center regularly boasted some of the company's top sales numbers, which made it even more difficult for Jeff to win Stephen over. "The kinds of things you are talking about may be great for trainees or for people who need a little extra encouragement to do their jobs well, but that's not the kind of operation I run here," Stephen told Jeff matter-of-factly. "*My* people are top professionals and what *my* people are motivated by is money. That's what makes them star salespeople after all and that's why *my* division always comes out on top."

Stephen's reaction put Jeff in a tough spot. It's hard to argue when someone is at the top of his game, and Stephen was one of the company's top performers. Jeff needed Stephen on his side. He couldn't afford to lose a top earner when the organization was underperforming so badly, so he had to tread lightly. He didn't want to force a confrontation that would turn off Stephen, but he also didn't agree with everything he was saying. It reminded him of something else his grandfather used to say: "Everyone needs a little coaching, no matter how good they think they are. And if it's good coaching, they'll thank you for it one day because everyone wants to be better at what they do."

Jeff decided to take that advice to heart and appeal to the director's sense of pride in his success.

"I recognize the fact that you're doing very well here," Jeff said to Stephen. "You deserve a lot of credit for consistently making this group among the top earners in the entire company. I'm sure that hasn't been easy in the current climate with so much competition from so many different places."

The director beamed at the praise, and Jeff let him enjoy it for a moment before he issued his challenge. "But my question to you is this: Could you be doing even better?"

The director looked surprised, so Jeff continued. "I'd like you to call Manuel in Chicago so he can tell you about what's he's been doing to raise the level of performance in his sales department. His efforts have managed to inspire some of his top salespeople to top even themselves. We had one standout last month who doubled her sales quota, and this month she's on track to do it again."

That piqued the director's interest and he promised to call Manuel the very next morning to find out more.

Jeff faced another challenge when he visited one of the company offices in India, where Samir, the well-intentioned facility manager, had arranged a recognition ceremony to coincide with Jeff's visit. As Jeff watched an older gentleman being presented with a gold-painted replica of the building they were standing in, he felt that something wasn't quite right. Maybe it was the lack of enthusiasm from the crowd or from the recipient himself, but when the ceremony was over, Jeff purposely avoided Samir and talked instead with some of the employees to try to get a better sense of what was going on.

When Jeff asked the people he met why this particular man was receiving an award, he wasn't very happy with the answers he received. "He's been here for a long time," seemed to be the best thing people had to say about him. When Jeff followed up by asking if they'd learned something valuable from his many years of experience or if he excelled in a particular area of the job, the responses he got were vague and uncomfortable. Everyone agreed he was a nice enough man, but it seemed unlikely that he was great at his job.

Afterward, Jeff met with Samir in his office. Jeff wasn't as angry or disappointed with Samir as he was frustrated that he hadn't been clear enough about the reasons behind recognition when he first introduced the idea. Still, he needed to nip the problem in the bud, so he said to Samir, "How did you choose the person who received your award today?"

"I chose him because he is the senior-most member of our team," Samir replied. "He has given many years of service to the company. He's been here even longer than I have."

"But has he done something recently that has made him stand out among the other employees? Has he gone above and beyond to help this facility achieve its goals?"

"He is a very reliable employee. He shows up every day without fail. He's nearly always on time," Samir replied.

It was then that Jeff made a mental note to add a new Guiding Principle to their list: "Make recognition a catalyst for results." This was not just about kind words and good feelings. It was very much about results—about rewarding and encouraging the kind of results the company needed to succeed. He shouldn't have assumed that idea would be obvious to everyone when his team had created their initial list of Guiding Principles. After all, even some members of his team had struggled with this one.

Jeff then explained to Samir that the point of recognition was to drive results, and that meant people should be recognized not because they had been around the longest or held a senior position, but for specific accomplishments that helped the organization reach its goals. "It's not that I don't appreciate someone who has stuck with this company for a long time, but I think the right time to recognize tenure would be at a retirement party. The point of making recognition a way of life in this organization is to drive results. Reward someone for just showing up every day, and you send the wrong message about what matters most to you as their leader, and to the company as a whole. Results are what matter above anything else, even seniority," Jeff told Samir. Samir was disappointed that Jeff wasn't more impressed with his ceremony, but he seemed to understand what Jeff was getting at

From there, Jeff went on to Australia, where he encountered a version of recognition that actually made him furious.

When Jeff first met Bruce, the head of their Australian business unit, he was treated to a lot of pomp and circumstance about their facilities and the efficiency of their operations, but there was no mention of recognition. When Jeff finally asked him what he was doing to make recognition a priority in his unit, Bruce deferred to his head of HR, who showed Jeff a collection of what looked like colored business cards printed with the words, "O Great One! Thanks for your contribution!"

"Bruce has tasked us with handing out these cards at least three times a week," the HR director told him.

Jeff stared at the cards dumbfoundedly. He couldn't think of a better example of what *not* to do when it came to showing people you valued and appreciated them. But he knew the fault didn't lie with the HR director, so he turned his attention back to Bruce.

"Do you mean to tell me that you've delegated recognition to your HR department? And that you're actually making it mandatory that they use these little cards three times a week?"

Bruce looked surprised by the question. "I wanted to make sure it got done," he responded.

"Bruce, I have to tell you, forcing people to appreciate one another is not what I had in mind when I introduced this idea. In fact, that's the last thing we want to do. We want recognition to be given because it's *deserved,* not because someone in HR has a quota to meet."

Bruce took a deep breath, and Jeff wasn't sure whether he was angry or just thinking about what he'd said. Finally, Bruce looked at Jeff and told him, "You're right. You're absolutely right." With that he took the recognition cards from his HR director and threw them in a nearby trash can. "When it comes to recognition, it looks as if we need to start over from scratch," he said.

To drive his point home, Jeff added, "'We' is the operative word here. Everyone needs to be involved, but you need to lead the way. You need to make sure that when recognition is given by you or by the people under you, it's sponta- neous, from the heart, and always tied to real accomplish- ments that produce genuine results. That's the only way it will make a real difference."

As Jeff was leaving, he told Bruce he'd follow up to find out what his new plans were for recognition, just as he'd done with Samir. It was starting to seem that the more places he visited, the more work he needed to do. After all, if everyone approached recognition in the same way that Samir and Bruce had, then the whole effort would founder. Recognition for recognition's sake simply wasn't going to help the company.

Through it all Jeff had to keep reminding himself to have the courage of his convictions. "Do the right thing and the right thing will happen," as his grandfather had said. He thought of that sentiment often as he explained over and over again, to group after group, what recognition meant and why it mattered. Even when things looked bleak, he knew the best thing he could do was to keep going, keep reinforcing his message, and keep believing that if he just set up the right environment for success, then real results would soon follow. He was just hoping that wasn't wishful thinking. The company needed a breakthrough and they needed it fast. The big question was where would it come from?

Chapter 27

Jeff's belief in recognition was finally rewarded during one of his trips back to Chicago. Because there was so much going on with the company overall, Jeff was regularly breaking up his round-the-world tour with frequent stops in Chicago to make sure his people there were still making recognition a top priority and that they weren't falling into the one-and-done trap that Dan once had. Of course he also had all the other aspects of running a business to keep up with as well.

Early one morning, Jeff was in his office busily trying to catch up on all he'd missed while he was away when Marjorie popped her head in to announce an unexpected visitor. "Dan is here to see you. Do you have time?" she asked.

Their meeting wasn't on the books, but Jeff had been keeping tabs on Dan's progress since his COO's recent missteps. He didn't want to miss an opportunity to coach him and make sure he was staying on course, so he told Marjorie, "Sure, send him in." As he said it, he tried to ignore the mountain of work sitting in front of him.

When Dan walked into Jeff's office, he looked as if he were ready to burst.

"Sorry to barge in on you like this. I just stumbled upon something, and I couldn't wait for the next team meeting. And I wanted to make sure I caught you before you left town again," Dan said.

"Not a problem, Dan. My door is always open. What've you got?"

"I did what you suggested and posted our Guiding Principles on the wall next to my computer. Every morning, when I get to the office, I read through them. I've gotten into the habit of picking one, and then, as my computer boots up, spending a few minutes trying to think up ways to make it real in my department. It has become something of a morning ritual."

"That's great. I'm really glad to hear it," Jeff said and he meant it. Part of him had still been wondering whether Dan had what it takes to lead operations, but he really wanted him to succeed despite his past stumbles.

"Thanks. It's definitely helped me focus. And it's also led me to something that I think could be big."

"Really?" Jeff said, unsure where this was going. "What's that?"

"Yesterday morning I was looking at Principle Number Three: 'A great idea can come from anywhere,' and I realized I hadn't done much to actualize that one in my department. I've had an easier time with the others. My department has been having more events and celebrations, just more fun together in general. I find opportunities to informally recognize people for doing good work practically every day, and I see leaders under me doing the same. I think I've become a better listener too. Even my wife said something about it the other day."

"That's definitely a good sign," Jeff smiled.

"I feel like my people are getting it. They know I care, and they are much more engaged in what they're doing as a result."

"That's fantastic!" Jeff told him.

"Yes, it is. I think it's been as rewarding for me as it has been for anyone else."

"That's the beauty of recognition," Jeff said. "It really does make everyone feel good, giver and receiver alike."

"Yes, but then there was that last principle: 'A good idea can come from anywhere.' Something about it kept nagging at me. I kept looking at it and wondering why I was finding it so hard to do something about it."

"Have you come up with something?"

"I have," Dan said, looking pleased with himself. "As I was sitting there yesterday morning staring at that principle,

I suddenly remembered something that happened back in Cleveland. Do you remember that engineer—her name was Julie—who talked about all the new product ideas her team had come up with? She had sent them over to our product development department, one after another, but never heard back about a single one. She said it was like sending messages into a black hole."

"I do remember that," Jeff said. He was suddenly even more interested in where this was going.

"That memory struck me like a bolt of lightning yesterday. So I went to Martin, who heads our product development department, and asked him to dig them out. He found them and then yesterday afternoon we went through them together."

"And?"

"I don't want to get too ahead of myself, but I think we may have struck gold!"

"Really? What were the ideas?"

"Martin and I talked to Julie this morning, and we were able to start formulating what I think is a viable strategy for bringing our signature product, Crazy Paste, into the twenty-first century. I really believe we can make this a truly iconic product once again. Not just of the past, but of the future. And the best part is, I think we can do it quickly."

Jeff stared at Dan for a moment trying to take in everything he was saying. He had always known that the principle Peter had added at the last minute was a good one, but he hadn't realized just *how* good until now.

"Our plan is a bit involved, so I'll need some time to take you through it. Maybe we can set up an appointment for some time this week before you leave town again?"

"I don't think I can wait that long, Dan," Jeff replied. "Let me talk to Marjorie about clearing my calendar for the next couple hours so we can do this right now. If this idea is as good as you say it is, we have no time to waste."

Chapter 28

Dan had been right about striking gold. Over the coming months, the team worked tirelessly developing a plan to make Crazy Paste a market leader once again.

The ideas Julie and her team had come up with for Crazy Paste involved improving the product and making it more relevant and appealing to today's kids. They were going to add cool new colors, some of which glowed in the dark or spontaneously changed when they came into contact with one another (they were calling these Chameleon Colors). They planned to introduce Crazy Paste Molds that made it easy for kids to create recognizable forms and were working on partnering with the producers of popular cartoons and movies to create molds of well-known characters. Julie's team had even come up with an idea for a Crazy Paste app that would turn photographs of people into Crazy Paste versions of themselves. The plan was to offer the app free to promote the new product line. There seemed to be no end to the possibilities of Crazy Paste 2.0. The whole idea, as soon as Dan introduced it, had immediately taken flight.

The entire team was now involved in making this the next big product for Happy Face Toys. Things had been going so well that they were banking on this being the product that would lift the company out of its slump. Nicole was working on the budget, Manuel was strategizing the launch, Anna had dedicated her best programmers to developing the app, and Peter was filing the patents. And the team in Cleveland, under Julie's direction, was already producing prototypes. It was all hands on deck, and Jeff couldn't imagine his team working harder or being more motivated to succeed than they were at that moment.

Jeff hated to miss out on all the excitement, but he also knew there was no better time than the present to continue his travels. The team had momentum and they knew what they were doing. They were working well together, and they had each other to turn to if they hit a stumbling block. It had been great to be a part of it all, but Jeff knew he was needed more elsewhere. Happy Face Toys was about a lot more than just what was happening in Chicago and Cleveland. He needed to keep driving his message home in more and more places around the world.

Jeff went on to introduce recognition to Happy Face employees from Mexico to the South Pacific. He encountered his fair share of skepticism, but he also found that if he just got people to voice their concerns and listened carefully to them, then he could begin to change their minds. *The best way to show people you care is to listen to them.* And when he was able to show people he cared, they suddenly became much more open to listening to his ideas in return.

Jeff hit what was probably his biggest stumbling block to date while he was in China visiting one of their manufacturing plants. He could tell the plant manager had his reservations when Jeff told him about all the different ways recognition was taking shape in different parts of the company, so he asked him what his concerns were.

The plant manager hesitated to contradict his CEO, but after some further prompting, he finally said to Jeff, "I can understand how this might work in Chicago and how it might work in Europe, but I believe recognition is a concept that's just too Western for the people here. Our culture is very different from yours. We're much more formal and we take our leaders very seriously. We believe they must always show strength, so giving out a funny award would be frowned upon. It just won't be taken seriously."

Jeff assured the plant manager that he'd meant what he said when he talked about the Guiding Principle of making it personal. "You know your people better than anyone else, better than I do certainly, so I trust you will come up with something that has meaning to them and still feels appropriate to you as their leader."

But the plant manager continued to have his doubts. He just didn't see recognition in any form as something his people would respond to, or even understand.

Jeff decided the best thing he could do was to give his presentation to the entire plant just as he'd planned, and then see how everyone reacted. The manager was reluctant, but at Jeff's insistence, he had all his workers stop what they were doing so Jeff could address the factory floor. As Jeff stood before them, many of the workers were clearly surprised to see their CEO. They looked a bit lost, and even a little confused as they stood staring back at Jeff, waiting to see what would happen. Jeff couldn't help but wonder for a brief moment whether the manager had been right, but there was no backing out now, so he launched into his speech.

Jeff started out by explaining the concept of recognition and talking about all the different awards company leaders were giving out around the world to recognize good work. He'd even brought along a visual aid—his very own OGO jar—which he kept hidden in a box until he was ready to reveal it to the crowd. As soon as he pulled it out and held it up for everyone to see, he was immediately met with waves of laughter. And he knew these were laughs of appreciation, not the derision the plant manager had predicted.

Emboldened by the response, Jeff delivered the rest of his speech with even more energy and conviction. When he got to the line that said, "Every person, no matter what they do, no matter how old or young, no matter how junior or senior, everyone deserves to be appreciated for contributing to all our efforts," the entire group spontaneously burst into applause. When Jeff delivered the final line, "No one in this world can succeed alone," they even gave him a standing ovation.

Moments like that one strengthened Jeff's resolve, and he worked hard not to let the disappointments shake his purpose. He believed strongly that his vision was right for the company and, on a grander scale, that it was simply the right way to treat people. He knew recognition could work because he'd seen it. Back in Chicago and in Cleveland, he'd seen recognition create the kind of environment where people were motivated and engaged, innovative ideas floated to the surface, and people worked together to make big things happen.

There were also moments when people truly inspired him even beyond his greatest expectations, like during the visit he'd paid to Nigel, who managed technical support for their European offices. Nigel worked closely with

Anna, and she had already told him about the success of her Top Scorer Award. With that in mind, Nigel had decided to try something of his own. He had rigged up an LED board in the departmental lounge that regularly flashed the name of their top-ranking support technician, followed by the words "Thank you for your support!!!" After those words had flashed a few times, they dissolved into an LED version of a fireworks display. It was an amazing demonstration of creativity that really brought the concept of recognition to life. But that wasn't even the best part. When Jeff visited, he noticed that anyone who happened to be passing by when the board flashed would clap hands and shout out the person's name that was flashing. "They just started doing that all on their own, completely spontaneously, to show their appreciation for their colleagues," Nigel told him with pride. Jeff couldn't think of a better example of the exponential power of recognition— not only does it inspire people to do great things, it also teaches them how to inspire others to do the same.

On the flight home, Jeff thought back on his experiences and was even more inspired. He wanted to add yet another Guiding Principle to the list: "Recognition is universal." Despite the pushback he'd received in various places and the missteps that had occurred in rolling out the idea, he had yet to witness a single person anywhere in the world, regardless of position or culture, who didn't like being recognized for doing good work. Thanks to his round-the-world tour of Happy Face offices and facilities, he now knew for certain something that he'd suspected all along: *Everyone wants to be appreciated for a job well done.*

The big questions left in his mind were whether appreciation would lead to the kind of results he was expecting, and whether those results would come fast enough to impress his board of directors. After all, his first year as CEO would soon be coming to a close.

Chapter 29

While Jeff was traveling the globe, Crazy Paste 2.0 was taking off in test markets. Customers loved the idea and initial sales results were more than promising, even surpassing expectations, which the team happily revealed to Jeff during one of his stopovers back in Chicago. They were ready for a full-scale launch of the new product line, and everyone was bristling with excitement.

Jeff, in turn, updated them on some of the experiences he'd had during his travels and on the two new Guiding Principles he'd been inspired to add to their list: "Make recognition a catalyst for results" and "Recognition is universal."

"I'm glad to hear that Nigel's team is really rallying around the concept of recognition," Anna said after listening to Jeff's update. "Their most recent customer satisfaction scores were significantly higher than in previous quarters, and I'm sure that has something to do with it."

She paused then and looked at Jeff seriously. "But it sounds like overall, your trip was pretty tough at times."

"It had its difficult moments," Jeff agreed.

"I hope we weren't that tough on you when you first introduced the idea to us," Anna said sheepishly.

It was her version of an apology for their run-ins of the past. Jeff knew it and he appreciated it. Things really had changed for the better.

Jeff appreciated Anna's concern, but he didn't want to dwell on the negatives. They were poised to accomplish big things, and that was where their focus should be. Besides, the trip had been challenging, but it had also been faith building at the same time, and he really wanted his team to see that.

"It certainly wasn't an easy trip," Jeff began, choosing his words carefully, "but nothing worthwhile is ever easy. This is a new way of thinking for a lot of people and change takes time, even for people who understand why they should change. I expected that. And seeing firsthand the reaction to recognition from so many different people in so many different places was a real learning experience for me. I would never have come up with these two additional Guiding Principles, for example, if I hadn't seen for myself some of the problems people were having. And I think they're really valuable additions."

"They are," Dan agreed. "I can't believe we didn't

include a principle tying recognition to results before now. I feel like we really missed the boat on that one."

Jeff was pleased to hear his COO talk like this. Dan had really come into his own in recent weeks. He had spearheaded the development of their new product line and done a great job with it. Jeff had kept in close contact with Dan while he was on the road so he could help him keep his focus where it needed to be. And Dan had done so. Jeff had made sure his COO knew how impressed he was with his progress, and Dan seemed to be displaying a new level of confidence as a result.

"There's always something more to learn," Jeff said. "That's part of the fun of doing business. Besides, at the end of the day, as difficult as it may have been at times, I always came back to the same thought: giving recognition is a true privilege, not a job. I'm in a position where I'm able to do this for people from all walks of life, all around the world. I get a chance to witness not just the setbacks, but also the exponential power of giving that not only inspires people to do great things, it also teaches them how to inspire the same in others. That's how momentum has built here with Crazy Paste 2.0, and it's how it will build throughout the Happy Face Toy Company. We just have to keep reinforcing the idea until it happens. And then reinforce it some more so it keeps happening."

"I think you may have inadvertently come up with another Guiding Principle to add to our list," Nicole said.

"What's that?" Jeff asked.

"Giving recognition is a privilege," she said. "I think that's an important thing to say. The truth is that fostering a spirit of recognition within my department has been the best part of my job. I love it and really feel privileged that I'm in a position to do that."

"I think we've all felt that. It's been as good for me personally as it's been for the business," Manuel added.

The others voiced their agreement.

Jeff smiled and looked at his team. Just a few months earlier he wouldn't have imagined such a dialogue happening among the people in this room. They sure had come a long way quickly. He wished he could take credit for the change, but he believed most of it belonged to them for having the courage to try something new and to the power of recognition to make a real difference. And it was a difference that would soon be felt throughout the entire company when the sales figures from their new product line started to come in.

Chapter 30

A few months after the full-scale launch of their new Crazy Paste product line, Jeff was back in his Chicago office early one Monday morning trying to catch up on some work. He had completed his round-the-world tour of the company, promoting recognition to as many people as he could, and was now looking forward to being back at headquarters with his team for a while. But he couldn't focus on what was in front of him. He kept thinking about the meeting he had scheduled for later that morning. His most difficult board member, Art, had called the week before to say he wanted to come by for a chat. That was all Art had said, and for the life of him, Jeff couldn't imagine what Art wanted to talk to him about in private.

When Art finally arrived about an hour later, he breezed right past Marjorie without even a glance at her. Then he walked right into Jeff's office as if he owned the place. Marjorie quickly got up and followed him inside. "I guess you can see that Art's here," Marjorie said to Jeff with an anxious look on her face.

Jeff just shook his head at Art's behavior. Jeff's grandfather had always made a point of treating everyone equally even though he was head of the company. When he wanted to point out the importance of treating all people, regardless of position, with courtesy and respect, he would say, "Don't look up, don't look down, always look straight ahead." Apparently Art didn't subscribe to the same philosophy.

"Thanks Marjorie, I've got it," Jeff said, smiling to let her know everything was OK. She gave Jeff a "good luck" look behind Art's back, and then left the room, closing the door behind her.

"Hi Art, what can I do for you," Jeff said evenly.

"Well, it was really Jennifer who wanted me to come by. She basically insisted. In advance of our annual board meeting next week, the board members had a conference call, and we've come to a decision. We know that you're going to Cleveland later today, so Jennifer thought it was important to tell you about it before you got there."

"What is it?" Jeff asked, readying himself for the other shoe to drop.

"Well, we've looked at the sales reports from the new products, and we have to admit, we were pleasantly surprised. Don't get me wrong, *I* still think the company has a long way to go. But we talked about it, and we're pleased with the progress you've made so far. So, you know, we'd like to ask you to stick around."

Jeff felt a wave of relief wash over him. He took a moment before turning his attention back to Art, who had sounded so uncomfortable delivering the news that Jeff almost wanted to laugh at him. He also wanted to say "I told you so," but he decided to take the high ground instead.

"Well, thank you, Art, and thank you to the rest of the board for continuing to put your confidence in me. I want you to know that I don't take it for granted. I realize that the company's journey has just begun."

Art nodded curtly at Jeff. Having said what he'd come there to say, he couldn't get out of Jeff's office fast enough. As soon as he'd gone, Marjorie appeared in the doorway.

"What was that all about?" she asked, looking at Jeff with concern.

"Believe it or not, he came here to tell me that the board would like me to keep my job."

Marjorie hooted with laughter at that. "Well, it took them long enough," she said. "How do you feel?"

"I feel . . . good," Jeff said slowly. "I mean, I wasn't expecting this news today, but it's certainly a relief."

"You must feel pretty happy too, right?" she prompted.

"Yes, of course," he said. "I'm happy. For myself but

even more for the people I have the privilege to lead. This is really a testament to all they've accomplished."

"Sometimes you remind me so much of your father," Marjorie said. "He never liked taking too much credit either."

"I think I'll take that as a compliment," Jeff said.

"Well, I think congratulations are in order. You deserve it," Marjorie said, beaming at him.

"Thanks," Jeff said. And then, as Marjorie was turning to leave, he added, "Hey Marjorie? Let's keep this to ourselves for now. I don't want anything to distract from the celebration today."

"Sure thing, coach," she called over her shoulder as she settled back in at her desk. "Whatever you say."

Jeff smiled at her use of the word "coach." He'd always felt that "boss" was for old-school leaders, a thing of the past. Calling him coach was one of the best compliments she could give him.

♔ ♔ ♔

Later that afternoon, the entire executive team—including Peter, who was no longer interim head of the legal department but had proved himself capable of taking over Adam's position—headed to Cleveland to celebrate the successful launch of Crazy Paste 2.0. When they arrived, they went straight to what was now starting to feel like familiar territory to Jeff: the warehouse. Only this time the warehouse looked like a whole new place. It was decked out in Crazy Paste–themed decorations for the party. There were elaborate Crazy Paste sculptures on the food table, streamers hanging from the ceiling in Crazy Paste colors, and lining the walls there were even Crazy Paste photos of Cleveland employees made with the Crazy Paste app. The people of Cleveland had gone all out for this event. They had finally fixed the Happy Face Toys sign out front like Jeff had asked them to and even adorned it with enormous Crazy Paste figures for the occasion.

Doug, Gabriel, and Julie were all there to greet Jeff's team when they arrived, and the celebration got started soon after. Dan kicked things off by presenting his Ace Navigator award to Julie and recognizing her and her team for coming up with the ideas behind their new product line. Manuel followed by announcing their most recent sales figures, which were stellar and made everyone cheer. And Julie wrapped things up with a presentation about where they planned to take Crazy Paste in the future. After that, everyone was ready to celebrate.

Jeff had purposely taken a backseat during the presentations, not wanting to upstage the contributions of those who were most responsible for making the new product line a success. Instead, he got a chance to hang back and survey the scene. His Chicago team was mixing easily with the Cleveland employees. All around him, he overheard people thanking and crediting each other for the work they had done. Everyone seemed genuinely happy, optimistic, and pleased to be a part of this celebration. Jeff couldn't ask for more. The company was far from perfect and they still had a lot of work to do, but he wasn't worried anymore. There was a new spirit alive and well at the Happy Face Toy Company, and he knew it would allow them to generate new ideas and solve problems together well into the future.

Jeff was lost in thought when the noise in the room suddenly died down. Jeff looked up and saw his entire team, along with Doug, Gabriel, and Julie, standing on the platform and looking his way. It was Dan who spoke first.

"As you all know, Jeff started as our CEO just over a year ago now. Many of you also know that when he took this job, he told the board of directors to give him a year to turn things around. He even invited them to fire him at the end of that year if they weren't happy with his progress. I always thought that was a bold move, and I'm happy to report that it paid off. The board has made their decision: They voted yesterday to keep Jeff on as our CEO!"

The crowd erupted in applause. Jeff was stunned. He

hadn't planned to tell his team about the board's decision until their meeting the following week. It must have been Marjorie who spilled the beans.

When the applause died down, it was Nicole who continued. "Jeff, we wanted you to know that we couldn't be happier or more proud to have you as our leader. We'd like to invite you to join us up here on stage because we have something we'd like to give you."

As Jeff made his way to the front, Manuel took over. "When Jeff first introduced the idea of recognition to us at a team meeting, he showed us something his grandson had given him. He called it his OGO jar. OGO stands for O Great One, which is what his grandson has always called him. We didn't realize it at the time, but that OGO jar was the start of a real sea change for this company, and one that we're all better for."

Jeff had made his way to the stage by then, and it was Anna who approached him now. "In the spirit of that OGO jar, we'd like to present Jeff with an award of our own. He is our OGO, our O Great One, the person who believed in us even when we gave him a hard time, the person who led us to become better at what we do and better people in the process. Jeff, this is our OGO award for you."

With that, she pulled something out of a box and held it out in Jeff's direction. It was a giant clapping chicken called Mr. Cluck, which had been one of his grandfather's first toy ideas. Once wound up, the toy would squawk and clap its big feathery wings, which was what it was doing as Anna passed the toy to Jeff. This Mr. Cluck was unique, however, in that it was wearing a T-shirt that had been custom made for the occasion. On the front it read in big block letters, "O Great One!" As Jeff stepped forward to receive the clapping chicken, he saw that the entire room was clapping along with it.

It was an emotional moment for Jeff, and he was as touched now as he had been when he'd received the OGO jar from his family. When he turned to address the crowd, he was more than a little choked up. But he quickly gathered himself together and spoke off the cuff and from the heart.

"When I first arrived at this facility as your new CEO nearly a year ago, I wasn't sure what to think. I witnessed the broken-down sign out front, I saw that dusty old trophy case with no Employee of the Month featured in years, and I heard people yelling at each other right here in this warehouse. I listened to you all tell me about problem after problem with no solutions in sight. By the end of the day, I really wasn't sure how we were going to get past all that. I wasn't even sure if we could."

Jeff paused for a moment and then flashed a huge smile. "But just look at us here today, at how far we've come in such a short amount of time, at what a different place this is now. When I first introduced the idea of recognition to this company nearly a year ago, there were a lot of people who thought it was a disastrous idea. Some said we couldn't make recognition a priority and still hold people accountable, but we've shown them that that isn't true. Others said we shouldn't recognize people until we crossed the finish line, but we've seen that recognition actually helps keep people motivated and on track every step of the way. Still others said that recognition was a Western concept that wouldn't work in our offices around the globe, but I've seen it resonate with people in China and India . . . really everywhere we've tried it. And then there were those who said that if we gave people too much credit or appreciation, they would lose their edge, they would lose their drive to succeed. But you've all proved that the opposite is true. You're more fired up than ever!"

The crowd let Jeff know with their cheers that they agreed with him. He just stood for a moment and listened before continuing.

"The idea for using recognition to turn this place around came from my own family, it came from a gift my grandson gave me when I was feeling discouraged. Since then I've come to believe that recognition is such a powerful idea that you can use it anywhere—at work, at home, anywhere where people are lacking the encouragement they need to succeed. I have to tell you, when the board told me they were letting me keep my job, they credited the company's turnaround to the new products we've introduced. But I knew this turnaround was about a whole lot more than that. Our new products certainly got our sales figures moving in the right direction, but new ideas and innovation don't just come out of the blue. None of this would have happened if it hadn't been for the people in this room, and if it hadn't been for the power of recognition to keep you all motivated and invested in our shared success. Without all that, we never would have made it here. As far as I'm concerned, what really turned things around at the Happy Face Toy Company was nothing less than a triumph of the human spirit!"

The crowd burst into applause at that, and Jeff felt himself starting to get choked up again. Fortunately, he had some time to regain his composure because the applause lasted for several moments. When it died down, he took a deep breath and continued.

"Because of that, I want you all to know that I share this award with each and every one of you. We've all come such a long way over this past year, and it's been a truly inspiring journey. Watching the way you have all supported each other and celebrated one another's accomplishments has been one of the greatest gifts of my life. And I believe this is just the beginning for all of us. The best is yet to come!"

The crowd responded with cheers this time. It was clear they were as excited about their future as he was, and it was incredibly gratifying to Jeff to see that.

"As for this guy," Jeff continued, gesturing toward Mr. Cluck. "He's just the icing on the cake. He's going to motivate me even more to stick to this path we've just begun to walk together because I believe it's a truly important path to be on. Introducing recognition here at Happy Face has made it a better place to work. If there was more recognition in the world, I believe it would be a better place to live. After all, I have to admit, I like receiving recognition almost as much as I like giving it, and I think everyone else does too!"

The crowd laughed and gave him another round of applause.

"I think there's only one thing left for me to say," Jeff said, feeling truly humbled by the moment.

"*Thank you. Thanks to all of you.*"

Epilogue

Flying back home to Chicago after the Crazy Paste celebration was a very different experience from the first time the team had left Cleveland together. This time everyone was chatting happily, reliving the experiences of the day and congratulating each other on their success. And they had a lot to be happy about. It was the first time the company had made its sales and profit goals in years. Things were going so well, in fact, that they were considering hiring more people at the Cleveland plant instead of shutting it down.

As they discussed the company's bright future, Anna suddenly turned to Jeff. "Are you really going to put pictures of *every* person you give an OGO award to on your office walls?" she asked him.

"I said I would, didn't I?" Jeff answered, smiling.

"It looks like you might be with us for a long time,"

she answered back. "What happens when you run out of wall space?"

Jeff paused for a moment and thought about that. Then he looked at Anna and said, "I hope I do get a chance to recognize so many people that I run out of wall space. And if that happens, then I'll start putting pictures on the ceiling. I can't think of a better thing to look up to every day!"

Anna laughed out loud at that, and the conversation turned to how the others might highlight past winners of their awards. As they were talking, Manuel said to the group, "You know guys, I think we're still missing something."

"Oh yeah, what's that?" Jeff asked him.

"I think we need one last Guiding Principle," he said. "When you were thanking everyone in Cleveland at the end, I remembered something Nicole said the last time we were there. It really resonated with me at the time, but I had forgotten about it until just then. She said, 'The two most powerful words in the English language are "thank" and "you," and it doesn't cost you a thing to use them.' What that really says to me is that there are no excuses, no good reasons why anyone can't give recognition a try. After all, no matter who you are—even if you're not a leader in your department—you can always say thank you to someone. It's easy to do, it's free, and it can really make someone's day. If we had a company full of people saying thank you to each other all the time, just imagine what a difference that could make."

Jeff smiled, thinking about how nice it would be to come to work every day to an environment like that and what a positive impact it could have on the entire organization.

Anna added, "You know, it's always bugged me a little that we stopped at nine principles. It just seems like we should have an even ten. I think that's a perfect one to round out our list."

"What does everyone else think?" Jeff asked the group. They all readily agreed.

"Principle Number Ten it is then," Jeff said. "Say thank you every chance you get!"

Resources

10 Guiding Principles for Inspiring OGOs

Recognition, or showing genuine gratitude, is the greatest form of encouragement and inspiration. By following these key principles, you can use it to motivate the people around you, drive real results, and feed your soul and theirs—all at the same time!

Principle #1: People won't care about you if you don't care about them.

You have to show people you care about them before you do anything else or expect anything from them.

Principle #2: The best way to show people you care is to listen to them.

People won't believe you care about them if you don't take the time to hear and acknowledge what they have to say. Besides, you can safely assume that everyone knows something you don't, so everyone is worth listening to.

Principle #3: A great idea can come from anywhere.

Great ideas don't always come from the highest ranking or most experienced person in the room. In fact, most of the time, they don't. But great ideas are essential to the success of any organization, so they need to be sought out and supported. A good idea is simply a good idea no matter where it comes from, so view everyone as a potential source.

Principle #4: Recognize great work and great ideas whenever and wherever you see them.

Great leaders celebrate other people's ideas as much as, or even more than, their own and they do it in a way that's spontaneous, real, and from the heart. In fact, the more spontaneous you are, the better. Don't wait for monthly meetings or annual performance reviews to show people you appreciate the work they do or believe in an idea they've come up with. Opportunities to recognize good work happen all the time, so look for those opportunities and make them count.

Principle #5: Make recognition a catalyst for results.

This isn't about rewarding people just because they've stuck around for a long period of time. The reason you recognize someone has to be directly tied to the real-world goals and objectives that you or your organization are trying to achieve. Reward the right things and more of the right things will happen. Reward the wrong things and you send the wrong message about what matters most. And believing in recognition doesn't mean you let poor performance slide.

Principle #6: Make it fun.

Take the business seriously but not yourself. Everyone will want to be involved in recognition if you create shared experiences that are fun for everyone, and not just for the person being recognized.

Principle #7: Make it personal.

That is, make it personal to you *and* to the person you're recognizing. Don't just give out the typical certificate or plaque when you recognize someone's contributions. Putting your personal stamp on the award makes it more meaningful, memorable, and fun for you and for those around you. And make sure to personalize each award by being specific about what that person has done to earn it!

Principle #8: Recognition is universal.

No matter their age, status, or nationality, people love to be recognized for what they do well and who they are.

211

Principle #9: Giving recognition is a privilege.

Don't think of it as just another item on your to-do list as a leader or manager. When exercised in the right way, giving recognition is a privilege that feeds people's souls and makes them feel great about themselves. And by feeding the souls of others, you'll feed yours in return. It's as good for the giver as it is for the receiver!

Principle #10: Say thank you every chance you get.

The two most powerful words in the English language are "thank" and "you." They are easy to say, and it doesn't cost you a thing to use them—so use them often!

Who's *Your* OGO?

Think about who the OGOs have been in your life, and then ask yourself:

What person has had the biggest impact on my life and why?

What role has he or she played in getting me to the place where I am today?

What has that meant to me?

Whose OGO Are *You*?

Consider the stories on the previous pages, as well as your own OGO story, and then ask yourself:

What if I could have that kind of effect on someone else's career?

What if I could have that kind of effect on someone else's life?

What would that mean to me?

Acknowledgments

The foundation of this little story about the amazing power of recognition has been built by a number of people. First, I want to thank my mom and dad, Charles and Jean Novak, who have always been my biggest fans. Their constant support and encouragement have given me confidence to get outside my comfort zone throughout my life, writing this book being just one example. I also want to recognize my wife, Wendy, and daughter, Ashley. Wendy constantly cheers me on and offered several meaningful suggestions to improve this book's content. Ashley actually presented me with the first OGO jar on Father's Day 2014, which helped inspire me to create this story. Yes, it really is a story based on real events!

Additionally, I want to thank all my team members at Yum! Brands, especially the more than two thousand O Great Ones whom I have recognized with my Walk the Talk, Floppy Chicken, and Cheese Head awards over the past twenty-one years. It has been one of the great joys in my life to recognize your accomplishments, build a recognition-based work environment, and at the same time enjoy so much business success doing it.

Next, I want to thank Christa Bourg, who collaborated with me to write this book. She captured my voice, added so much value and creativity, and helped create a page-turner that my friends tell me they couldn't put down. Christa, you deserve OGO Award #1 for being such an outstanding talent and writer.

Last but not least, I want to thank God. For the life of me, I will never know why I've been allowed to live the life I have when I see so many others who are less fortunate. I'm truly humbled by it and feel so blessed to have found a vocation I can dedicate the rest of my life to: building awareness of the recognition deficit that exists in the world today and, hopefully, inspiring people to do something about it.

Thank you so much for reading this book and, more important, for using recognition to make a positive difference in the lives you touch.

A Note About
This Book

One hundred percent of the profits I receive from the sale of this book will be donated to the Wendy Novak Diabetes Center and other entities leading the fight against diabetes. I chose this charitable cause because my wife, Wendy, who is unquestionably the greatest OGO in my life, has lived with diabetes since she was seven years old. Her strength and resolve as she has fought the effects of this disease have always been an inspiration to me, our entire family, and so many others. Juvenile diabetes (T1D) is a devastating disease, and we must help people deal with its complications and find a cure.

Welcome to the World of OGO

I'm on a mission to get more people in the world to recognize others for being the great people they are and for doing the great things they do. I created the OGO brand with this purpose in mind. Just as Nike is known for bringing innovation and inspiration to athletes around the world, I want OGO to be known for turning the global recognition deficit into a surplus!

How Does OGO Do It?

We make it easy and fun by giving people ideas and products they can personalize to tell someone in their lives how great they are and how much they're appreciated. Our product line features the OGO J.A.R, the *Jackpot of Acknowledgment and Recognition*!

We challenge by asking, "Who's Your OGO?" We share peoples' personal stories of greatness, and in doing so, we inspire people to take action by recognizing and celebrating the great in everyone.

Why Does OGO Do It?

Because recognition makes people feel good.

Because recognition inspires people to be even more amazing.

Because recognition inspires people to do more great things.

Because more people doing more great things makes the world a better place.

OGOs Are Everywhere!

At work: employee, manager, assistant, partner, lunchroom staff, customer.

At home: dad, mom, son, daughter, grandma, grandpa, sister, brother, husband, wife.

In our everyday lives: teacher, doctor, firefighter, friend, boyfriend, girlfriend, coach, graduate.

OGO turns people on to the power of recognition by inspiring them, challenging them, and making it fun! For more on how you can join in OGO's mission and help make the world a better place, visit us at WhosYourOGO.com.

Share Your Stories

How has recognition affected you and the people around you? Too often we spend too much time focusing on the negative. Here's your chance to focus on the posi- tive and celebrate how recognition has made a powerful difference in your life and in the lives of people you know.

We want to hear from you! Share your personal OGO stories with us at WhosYourOGO.com.

Always looking for OGOs!

David Novak

To My OGO

Dedicate This Book to the OGO in Your Life

To my OGO: _____
You're my OGO because . . .

_____

_____

_____

_____

_____

_____

_____

_____

_____

_____

_____

_____